Before the Box

Freeing the Church to Emulate
First-Century Christianity

Jason Homan

ISBN: 1497406064
ISBN-13: 978-1497406063

DEDICATION

This book is dedicated to:
My parents L. Allen and Jerrie Homan. Their lives have been an example of a fervent and balanced walk with Jesus Christ.

My beautiful and talented wife Debbie who has been supportive through the many hours of working on this project.

BEFORE THE BOX – JASON HOMAN

CONTENTS

BEFORE THE BOX – JASON HOMAN

ACKNOWLEDGMENTS

Thanks to the friend of my youth and now servant of our Saviour, Jeff Lee who has been kind enough to lend his support in writing the foreword for this book.

Many thanks to those kind gentlemen who reviewed the book in its editing stages. Their help and advice on content was extremely valuable in this process.

FOREWORD

What would you do if you met a kid on the street who had a history of getting into trouble, had a dirty mouth and was not all that interested in God? Love him like Christ and step into his world and look for every opportunity to share the Gospel of Jesus Christ is the answer. That's exactly what Jason Homan did for me! He and his family showed the love of Jesus Christ, lived the Gospel, and shared it with me.

I was that trouble-making, foul-mouthed pagan on the street. In the summer of 1985, I met Jason Homan as a nine-, almost ten-, year old when they moved next door to my home. There was something very different about Jason and his family that made an impression on my life. I had grown up in a home where my mother was a Roman Catholic and my father was agnostic. I went occasionally to RC mass but never understood what Christianity was all about; it did not really effect my life at all. Then I met Jason and his family. Truly, they are a family that loved God and desired to live for Christ in every way. The manner by which they loved my family and others around them was second to none.

Due to their love toward our family, my mother and father for the first time, allowed the older siblings in our family to attend "Vacation Bible School" at Homans' church. It was there for the first time I heard the Gospel message that Jesus Christ died on the cross to pay the penalty for my sin, my offenses toward God and others. I needed to believe in Jesus Christ and what he had done on my behalf -- facing God's wrath for my sin, making atonement for me personally through his death -- and believe in His resurrection from the dead.

Since then, God has changed my life, plans, and desires. I am so very grateful to Jason, and his family for introducing me to Jesus Christ as my Saviour. Jason is a true friend who loves God, loves others, has a passion for the study of God's Word, and has a passion to share Christ with others.

In his book, "Before the Box," Jason attempts to analyze many different aspects of church, church life, and our Christian responsibilities, and to challenge our existing presumptions in these areas. You may not agree with all that Jason brings to the table in his book; but trust me, this work will help challenge you to expand that box of assumptions. It will challenge you from Scripture, and I pray draw you closer in relationship to the Lord and His Word, to bring Him glory and honour.

Rev. Jeffrey Lee
Church Planter/Evangelist, United Kingdom
Bringing Hope amongst Muslims and British

INTRODUCTION

The phrase "out of the box" has become one of the most over used clichés of the past decade. This book is not for those who are looking to grab an idea or two that are just outside of the mainstream and apply it to their church situation.

This book is for those who realize that the recent dramatic changes in popular mindset and culture have left us scrambling for relevance and that we are living within a box that for a great majority of congregations no longer fits. It is for those who wonder, "Has it always been this way?" It is for those who ask, "What was it like before the box?"

My goal is twofold. One goal is to get some things written down that I have been working on for a number of years. My second goal is to convince churches to quit trying to fit into a box and to start trying to fit better into the Book.

For clarification, when we talk about the "box", we are really talking about our traditions, expectations, and methods. Orthodox theology (that set of beliefs that makes up the core of true Christianity) is not up for debate. As a matter of fact, it is those core doctrines that are so needed today to face the challenging times in which we live.

In our day there are basically two camps. The "progressive/liberally-minded" churches have encased themselves into a box or a set of expectations and practice as expressed by their favourite preacher or teacher. This generally means that the loudest, most famous voice sets the agenda for the group. At the other end of the spectrum, the hyper-conservative/traditional congregations have done the same. Somewhere between these two boxes of dogma is a common-sense Biblical ground.

Unfortunately, the longer a church or movement exists, the more set in stone its operational structure and spiritual expectations become. Having downloaded this structure and these expectations into their spiritual lives, that denomination or group of churches begins to think as a group and shuts out all outside voices of dissension or opposition – even if they are Biblical and well-intended. At some point, some dear soul wanders just outside the box of these structures and expectations; takes a good long hard look at them, and wonders, "What would this congregation, this movement, be without the box?" That is the question we wish to explore together.

Let's face it; first-century Christianity (before the "box") looked very different from what we see in churches today across the spectrum of what we can loosely call Christianity. (I say that because much of what is happening, in both conservative and more "progressive" churches looks very little like Christ.)

We all realize that no church is perfect. Ideal is not something that we attain, but rather it is something for which we strive. Having said this, it is important for us to know what the ideal is. It is essential to know our goal for it determines our direction. It is my intention in the pages of this book to walk through the church with you and talk together about the ideal, about what a simple, Biblical dynamic could look like in a local church.

We often look for what is "new". Everyone, it seems, is looking for some new gadget, preacher, program, model, or theory to make their church more "successful". What I am advocating is not really all that new. I am asking us to take a look at the early church without the bias of our culture and religious traditionalism in order to emulate their strengths and to avoid their weaknesses.

As we walk through this book together, there will be some things on which we will agree, and some things about which we will have to disagree in love and with civility. In addition, there are other thoughts that will necessitate more thinking and time to come to a consensus.

Take what is helpful for you and leave the rest. But in the end, at least we get to put voice, context, and organization to a conversation that has been going on quietly within the churches for some time. The question is not, "Is my new box better than your old box?" The real question is, "Could we do without the box altogether like the first-century believers did, and how can we best glorify God and reach others for Jesus in this millennium?"

Throughout this book, I will challenge pre-conceived notions. Let me say at the outset that I have great appreciation for those who have come before me. They have given me the benefit of their years of experience with Christ, and for that, I am eternally grateful. However, each generation can only do the best they know. If this current generation of leadership in the church is wise they will encourage the next generation to go further than they themselves have gone with Christ. I would be a fool to think that I have God, the Bible, the church, and the Christian life all figured out. It is my earnest desire that those who come after me will go higher with God, understand Him and His church better, and be greater for God than me.

In the great span of time, I'm just one among a thousand recruits lined up on the parade field, wearing the uniform of the Kingdom that we all love and pledge to defend and to promote. It is my privilege to honour those great men of God, those generals, who have fought the battles and have led us to where we are today. I am humbled by the men that have preceded me and will ever be there to applaud their leadership of the churches through the centuries.

This, I suppose, is as good a place for the disclaimer as anywhere else in the book, so here it is:

Within this book, I attempt to describe the extremes of various positions so that we may come to an understanding or at least the beginning of a conversation toward a balanced, consistent, Biblical position. My descriptions of the extremes are not out of a heart of malice. These descriptions are necessary (even in their generality and sometimes caricature) to establish some kind of framework; some landmarks as it were, on a line of belief and practice.

I use, for the most part, generalities and broad sweeping macro statements that do not necessarily apply to every particular situation in the micro (although most of the time they do). This is not a book about specific trees and their characteristics, but rather, it is a bird's eye view of the forest. So, if you see yourself in one of these generalities or caricatures, I am not talking about you, but I am probably (read this: most definitely) talking to you. This is where a smiley face goes, but my editor won't let me use emoticons!!! May God bless you, and it is my desire that He may use some little thing from this book to help you, your family, or your church.

1. MOTIVE BEFORE THE BOX

We are all a product of what has come before us. As a young boy growing into a young preacher, most of what I heard concerning motivation was, "Love Jesus more, and you will be more motivated," and "Tell others of Jesus in order to keep people out of Hell. That's your motivation." While both of those are good goals and Biblical, they are not sufficient motivation. Why? Because they are centered around and dependent upon man as the source of motivation instead of upon God.

It wasn't until Bible college that I had a breakthrough in this area of motivation. Up until this point, I thought that my lack of motivation was due to a lack of love for Christ or for others. However, one day a down-to-earth preacher named Charles Keen[1] said that if we understood God's love for us, we would have no problem with our motivation in service to Him. This truth was revolutionary and has never left me. But we will get to that...first, the Great Commission.

To obey the Great Commission is one of the greatest privileges of the Christian in this present age. To show others that a God of love and mercy sent His Son to pay the penalty for our sin so that we might have the opportunity to receive forgiveness and a home in Heaven is an honour that we ought not take lightly. It comes as a bit of a surprise to us then, that in the very area that we need motivation, the verses that we refer to as the Great Commission give us a mandate and a method, but not a motive. Take a look:

Matthew 28:18-20 And Jesus came and spake unto them, saying, All power is given unto me in heaven and in earth. Go ye therefore, and teach all nations, baptizing them in the name of the Father, and of the Son, and of the Holy Ghost: Teaching them to observe all things whatsoever I have commanded you: and, lo, I am with you alway, even unto the end of the world. Amen.

In these verses:

- We find empowerment in the presence of Jesus. (vs. 18,20)
- We find a commission – a job to do – go, teach, baptize. (vs. 19)
- We find assumed results. ("Teaching them" – Teaching who? Those who have responded to the Gospel.)

What we don't find in this portion of Scripture is our motive. Why did Jesus leave that out? My contention is that He left it out because it was understood; it was such a central part of the fabric of first-century Christianity that it really didn't need to be spelled out. The crucifixion (God's display of the depth of His love) was freshly seared into the DNA of the young first-century church.

Motives are important. There is a story about a dog who was bragging that he was the fastest dog that ever was and the greatest hunter too. About that time a rabbit came hopping

2

by, and all of his doggie friends challenged him to chase and kill the rabbit. Well, to keep his little doggie ego inflated, he tore after the rabbit. After miles of chase, the now deflated doggie returned to his buddies. They ribbed him for not catching the rabbit. "Boys," he said, "It's all about motivation. I was running for my lunch, but the rabbit was running for his life."[2]

And so, the question becomes, dear reader, for what are you running? Is it a sufficient reason to keep running?

God cares about our motives.[3]
   Proverbs 21:2 Every way of a man is right in his own eyes: but the LORD pondereth the hearts.

Often, we plod ahead in the Christian life and ministry for reasons that are not necessarily bad but are insufficient as motivation to carry us through long term. Let's look together at a list of insufficient motivations and some thoughts regarding them.

Insufficient Motivation: I keep going to look good to others – to please man.

Ok, this should be an easy one to dispel.
Proverbs 29:25 says, "The fear of man bringeth a snare: but whoso putteth his trust in the LORD shall be safe."

And look at **Galatians 1:10, "For do I now persuade men, or God? or do I seek to please men? for if I yet pleased men, I should not be the servant of Christ."**

Of course, having this as a core motivation puts us in the position of trying to keep everyone happy. Eventually, because we cannot keep everyone happy, we burn ourselves out trying to do so.

This is especially true with missionaries and church planters because those in that position think that they have to keep all their supporting churches (and more particularly, the pastors and missions boards of those churches) happy. When man becomes our master instead of our partner, we are on our way to burnout and worse.

Insufficient Motivation: I keep going to keep from feeling guilty.

Acting out of guilt is the opposite of freedom. John 8:36 says, "If the Son therefore shall make you free, ye shall be free indeed"

Guilt is the prison cell of the sincere and well meaning. We all want to do well, and there is always something more to do in the ministry. That doesn't mean that it all can be (or even should be) done by you.

For some reason, we see God as an angry father that keeps demanding more instead of a loving father that is more concerned about us and our welfare than He is about the amount of work that we can get done for Him. Let that sink in; God is more concerned about your physical, emotional, and spiritual well-being than He is about your productivity.

Jesus died for you…not for your productivity. In the end, guilt leads to bitterness, anger, and resentment. It is a prison because we will never do enough to satisfy our guilt in what we imagine that God demands.

When we follow the path of guilt rather than prayer and

the leading of the Holy Spirit to show us what God has called and enabled us to do, we are on our way to trouble town.

Insufficient Motivation: I keep going because it is my duty.

Here is a catch twenty-two. There are times that we must plod on in duty, but duty is not a motivation in and of itself.

The soldier slogs through the blood and mud out of a duty that comes from a love of home and country. The father works the hot and dirty dead-end job out of a duty that comes from a love for his family.

Duty is not a motivation in itself; it is the implementation of a motivation. Simply to plod on because it is "what I do," or the "right thing to do," or "what has to be done," only ends in frustration, anger, and the pain of a broken heart. If duty is my main motivation, then I eventually find myself upset with the one who has dumped this duty upon me (friends, family, my church, even God). I feel put upon, overworked, undervalued, and underpaid. Duty without a sufficient motivation behind it is nothing more than volunteer slavery.

What then is our "duty?" *Let us hear the conclusion of the whole matter: Fear God, and keep his commandments: for this is the whole duty of man. For God shall bring every work into judgment, with every secret thing, whether it be good, or whether it be evil. (Ecclesiastes 12:13-14)*

What does the Bible mean when it talks about "His commandments?" Is God a taskmaster with a whip? Certainly not. Jesus has not come to enslave us to duty for duty's sake.

Remember He said, *"Take my yoke upon you, and learn of me; for I am meek and lowly in heart: and ye shall find rest unto your souls. For my yoke is easy, and my burden is light." (Matthew 11:29-30)*

Duty then is the outworking of a motivation, not a motivation in and of itself. When I work solely upon the basis of duty, it is as slippery as a winter hill on a crazy carpet...and just as dangerous.

Insufficient Motivation: I keep going to grow the church.

We all know that Jesus said, *"I will build my church" (Matthew 16:18)*

We remember that Paul said, *"I have planted, Apollos watered; but God gave the increase." (1 Corinthians 3:6)*

So why then are we all so obsessed with our own efforts? Having asked that question does not nullify our responsibility to be obedient to Scripture in the area of talking to others about the Gospel of Christ. But with thousands of church growth books flooding the market, don't you think that the pendulum has swung just a little too far (like WAY too far) toward human effort and ingenuity? Of course it has. We get so impressed with our ideas, our big new plans, and our work ethic, that we forget that it is, *"Not by might, nor by power, but by my spirit, saith the LORD of hosts." (Zechariah 4:6)*

A worldly philosophy obsessed with productivity, growth, and results has overwhelmed the churches in the last half century and even more so since the mega-church emphasis in the 1980's. A Biblical definition of success has been lost within the churches.

6

We need to remember that God is more concerned with our person than He is with our productivity. Jesus said that it is His job to build His church. We overestimate our influence when we in our pride think that we can take responsibility for church growth.

God has saved us to be worshippers first and workers somewhere way down the list. Yes, it is true that work (along with everything else in our life) is supposed to be part of our worship, but it is not the greatest part.

Because work is seen by man we give more time to it than private worship. Who are we trying to please anyway? We can't grow the church! We can advertise, preach, visit, promote, and pray. But to take the responsibility for church growth upon our shoulders is to set ourselves up for either disappointment and depression or for the self- congratulatory pride of "successes" who portray an attitude that conveys that their wisdom, methods, and works somehow eclipse that of God's work in the building of His church.

Insufficient Motivation: I keep going to save people from hell.

Okay, now I know that this thought may initially strike you as cold, offside, or even in error, but give me a minute and it will all make sense.

First, God sent Jesus to *"reconcile all things unto Himself." (Colossians 1:20)* The goal was God focused.

Everything is supposed to be God centered and directed toward God! *Romans 11:36* says, *"For of him, and through him, and to him, are all things: to whom be glory for ever. Amen."*

Avoiding the punishment of Hell was a fantastic byproduct (or if you don't like the word "byproduct", insert here "God ordained result") of our reconciliation to God. The reconciliation was God's primary aim.

We know that the privilege of having a part in saving people from eternal punishment is a valid reason for soulwinning. However, it is not the ultimate motivation, and there is a difference between a reason and a motivation.

If keeping people out of Hell becomes our sole motivation, it is insufficient, and we will quit.

An insufficient motivation is like a flat tire on a bike. You can ride it for a long distance, but you know there is a problem and eventually you have a very hard and bumpy ride on an out-of-round rim. Why isn't "keeping people out of Hell" enough of a motivation to sustain us? Simply put, it is because we are selfish beings.

Altruistic motives come in spurts. We see the abused animal or the starving child on the television, and we are spurred to action - maybe. Why? Because we are selfish people who have to be reminded of a need in order to act. We all know that there are abused animals and starving children in this world. Why don't we consistently help? Because we are selfish and altruism is not a sustainable motivation.

We know we should feel sympathy for a poor lost soul on his way to hell but because we are carnal, fallen, and selfish beings, we can't keep up a continuous stream of concern that will motivate us long term. Our own worries, concerns, and just plain day-to-day challenges quickly obliterate any "pitiful" feelings we may have toward the lost. Why? We don't love others enough for this to be a sufficient motivation. That's the cold hard truth.

For example, my wife has dogs. I like one of them. She is a cute, happy female that jumps up and licks me (the dog, that is) and is happy when I come home. The other one is a growly little mutt that I put up with because my wife loves him. I feed that dog, take him for walks, and pay good money at the vet for his care. Why? Because my wife loves the dog.

Okay, so when we move from the silly to the sanctified the principle is still the same. I really don't care about other people, but the God who loves me and who I love; loves them. Because He loves me, I choose to care about what He cares about and love who He loves.

So, because people are important to God, I choose to try to point them to His salvation. Saving people from Hell is not a wrong reason for evangelism; it's just an insufficient motive.

Insufficient Motivation: I keep going because there is no one else to do it, and it has to get done.

Does this sound familiar? So many good believers are involved in aspects of ministry for which they have no call, gifting, or empowerment, and they are miserable! There are parts of any job that we don't like to do. That's not what I am talking about.

What I am referring to is the pastor that thinks that he has to cut the church grass, or the Sunday School teacher that gets roped into doing the bulletins because, "There's no one else to do it." What a recipe for disaster! God wants us to have willing servant's hearts. But do not confuse a servant's heart with the will of God or the gifting of the Holy Spirit. (Just because there is no special music for Sunday morning, doesn't mean that tone deaf Uncle Sal needs to give it a try just so we can say we had someone sing a special number this week.)

Sometimes you just have to let things slide. Did I really say that? Yes! Do you really think that if you work really hard, and do everyone else's jobs that you can get it all done perfectly, and that God will bless with thousands saved because of your perfection?

If you do it all, what motivation will others have to fill their God-called roles and use their gifts? If the Holy Spirit isn't urging you to take on some task in the ministry, and you do it; you will just end up being bitter against those who "should be doing this." This is a trap of the devil (Yes, I know that "devil" is a proper name of a real person and should be capitalized, but I don't like the guy.) for those who truly care and want everything done and done right. The saying, "If you want something done right, do it yourself" is the pitfall of those who think that perfection in ministry is possible this side of heaven and is demanded of them by God.

You can't do it all. You will burn out, and a pile of ashes isn't much good to anyone. Henry Martyn[4] said, "Let me burn out for God." He was talking more about spending his whole being and life on service to Christ; (especially in the area of prayer) not about what we consider "burn out" today.

The idea of working ourselves into a physical or mental breakdown is not Jesus' idea of ***"ye shall find rest unto your souls. For my yoke is easy, and my burden is light." (Matt 11:29b-30)***

Insufficient Motivation: I keep going to see lives changed.

Okay, a couple of things here. First, every religion in the world changes lives. Man loves to feel superior, holy, and noble as a result of following rules. All religions have rules that if followed, generally make someone a better, kinder human being. But is it our job to make better, kinder lost people? No. Any minister, priest, rabbi, or imam could do that.

Jesus didn't come to alter the lives that we had by a little alteration here and there around the edges. He came to give us a new life and change us completely into new creatures. God wasn't interested in simple moral progress, He sent Jesus for something far more important. That is, radical renovation at a core level. He came to give life and life more abundant to people that had been transformed into new creatures.[5]

We rejoice in the drunkard's sobriety or the harlot's change in occupation. Instead of admiring the God of the change we tend to promote the change, and selfishly, our role in it. This is nothing more than self-promotion in a disguise and pride on display. The gospel changes people not by outward adherence to moral principles but through an inward revolution…what God calls a "new creature". God is creating a new race of people for a new Kingdom.

Secondly, the problem with using changed lives as motivation is that our concept of our own success or failure is then tied to someone else. If our converts show up at church, are evangelistic, tithe, kick their addictions, clean up their language, etc… (you know the drill) then we allow ourselves to feel the satisfaction of being a "success." If, however, those same converts take detours back toward the Kingdom of Darkness, then we feel their failure as our own.

We cannot take credit for another's success, and we certainly cannot take the blame or feel the guilt for another's failure. Our job is the faithful teaching of the Word. What others do with it (changed lives or not) is between them and God. To hook your wagon to the motivation of changed lives is equivalent to tying a balloon to a roller coaster...lots of ups and downs and eventually some bratty little kid pops your balloon.

Our All Sufficient Motivation

Paul was a guy who needed a solid foundation when it came to motivation. If we had to go through what Paul did, we wouldn't make it. What kept him going?

Look with me at *Second Corinthians 5:13-14*
"For whether we be beside ourselves, it is to God: or whether we be sober, it is for your cause. For the love of Christ constraineth us; because we thus judge, that if one died for all, then were all dead:"

Okay, so we finally get to a motivation that will sustain us...a motivation that is truly sufficient –the Love of God. Paul said that it was this love that "constrained" him.

Here is the Strong's[6] definition: "constrain" - to hold together, i.e. to compress or arrest (a prisoner); figuratively, to compel, perplex, afflict, preoccupy:—constrain, hold, keep in, press, lie sick of, stop, be in a strait, straiten, be taken with, throng.

Simply put, to constrain means to hold in place. If we are put in constraints that means someone has tied us up or put shackles on us. What then shackles the servant of God to his service? **The love of God.**

Admittedly, there is debate among scholars as to whether this passage is talking about God's love for us or our love for Him. Let me make the case for the former. Our love for God vacillates. God's love for us is constant.

Our love for God is a responsive love. It is like a thermometer that goes up and down depending upon the room temperature. God is the thermostat. He sets the temperature of love in our relationship, and that temperature is set on "high"! It is our role to respond to His love. Notice *First John 4:19 "We love him, because he first loved us."*

If our love for God comes from us it cannot motivate us. How can one be motivated by something which he himself produces? That is kind of like the artist showing you his painting and telling you that he was inspired to paint that painting by that same painting. Confusing, right? Yes, and it is the same circular logic that we have applied to our love for Christ. We cannot be inspired by our own love. It is a responsive love. However, His love, displayed ultimately upon the cross, is highly motivating.

My argument is that the more we come to understand God's love for us individually, the more we are motivated to please Him.

John 3:16 For God so loved the world, that he gave his only begotten Son, that whosoever believeth in him should not perish, but have everlasting life.

Motivation in ministry then goes something like this. "I see how much God loves me. Therefore, as an act of love toward Him, I will keep going." God has to be the motivation!!! Everything else falls flat eventually.

When we see God as both the end of our service and the motivation to that end we see a picture free of human selfishness, pride, and ego.

Romans 11:36 For of him, and through him, and to him, are all things: to whom be glory for ever. Amen.

Look again, please, at **Second Corinthians 5:13-14.**
"For whether we be beside ourselves, it is to God: or whether we be sober, it is for your cause. For the love of Christ constraineth us; because we thus judge, that if one died for all, then were all dead:"

In these verses, we see that ministry is "to God", "for others (your cause)", and "because of (and motivated by) Jesus (the love of Christ)". Even though others benefit from our ministry, they cannot be the motivation for our ministry. Ministry has to be totally "to God". The fact that others benefit from it has to be lower priority in our motivational structure, because God must be the priority.

What place then does the glory of God have in our motivation?

Ephesians 3:20-21 says, **"Unto him be glory in the church"**

The glory of God is, of course, a fallout from the motivation of love, not a motivation in itself. If we are motivated by the love of God for us, then we will love Him. If we love Him we will want Him to be seen as great in the eyes of others. You know, kind of like we want everyone to think well of our wife and kids…because we love our wife and kids.

We glorify (promote) what we love. We love (because of our human nature) in response to love (God's).

Where does pleasing God fit into correct motivation?

Revelation 4:11 tells us that we were created to please God.

Pleasing God, of course, is another effect of the landslide that is the love of God, not a motivation in itself.

Funny enough, we think that it is what we do that pleases Him instead of who we are. We think that He is more impressed with our production than He is in the person He is forming us to be. In thinking this way, we elevate our handiwork over the workmanship of God.

We exalt achievement and downplay character in our society. However, any parent worth their salt will tell you that they would rather have a godly teenager flipping burgers at the local fast food establishment than a rebellious teen heading up a dot-com empire. I think we have forgotten that God is a Father who is first interested in who we are, and then He helps us do what we do.

Did you ever read about God's inspection of Adam's work in the garden? We all think in the back of our minds that this is the reason why God was showing up in the "cool of the day" – to inspect. Nope, it was to spend time with the one who pleased Him. Adam didn't please God because of his own production, but instead Adam pleased God because Adam was God's creation!

God isn't nearly as excited about what we are doing (although we do right in response to His love) as He is excited about His new creation...what He has created in us and is doing in us! That is what He is pleased with.

The truth is that God is easily pleased. We do not work to be accepted by Him. We are already made acceptable by the blood of Jesus and are accepted on the basis of grace, not our own merit.

Ephesians 1:6 To the praise of the glory of his grace, wherein he hath made us accepted in the beloved.

He is pleased when He sees what He has done in us, not what we have done to look good to Him. Remember the ***"filthy rags"*** part? ***(Isa 64:6)*** It's what He does in me that matters!!!

For some tangled and bungled up reason we have this notion that we keep God happy by our works. We couldn't please Him with our works at salvation, and we aren't supposed to walk by works now. ***(2 Cor. 5:7)***

Oh, how much pain we cause ourselves when we have a distorted view of God. So many times we see Him as a quality inspector on an assembly line instead of as a grandparent waiting for the grandchildren to arrive for a visit. Let's look at it from a purely human perspective for a moment. If your son was killed protecting the life of your grandchild, wouldn't it warm your heart to see little reminders of your son in your grandchild's features, speech, and actions? Sure it would. Seeing Christ in us; that's what pleases our Heavenly Father. We aren't made pleasing to God by our actions. We are made acceptable and pleasing to God by the blood and the cross of

Jesus.

Does this mean we don't do our best? Does this mean we should not try to live holy and exemplary lives? Does this mean that God doesn't care at all about the quality of our work? I did not say any of those things. But the thing that God is most concerned with is, *"My little children, of whom I travail in birth again until Christ be formed in you," (Galatians 4:19)*

2. INNER SPIRITUAL LIFE BEFORE THE BOX

When it comes to one's inner spiritual life, it seems that there are several "boxes" to which people resort. Usually this is dependent upon their temperament, training, and tradition.

The first "box" would be that of the academic. The academic approach to the spiritual life is for many, the standard. This devotional structure is mostly made up of the basics of read the Bible, memorize the Bible, and pray. If, however, God happens to want more out of our relationship than ten or twenty minutes in the morning reading a devotional guide and giving Him our want list, then we have some work to do creating a new (or rather an old) Biblically-based toolbox for our inner spiritual life.

At the opposite end of the playing field upon which we find ourselves is the "experiential" team. For this group of people feelings are paramount. In their pursuit of a "God encounter" they make much of worship and feelings but very little of the systematic study and application of the Scriptures. This craving for an experience above a desire for the bread of the Word of God leaves them feeling empty and always looking for the next spiritual high. Unfortunately, when emotion becomes the barometer of that "spiritual high" it becomes easy to counterfeit and manipulate people into believing that they have had a spiritual experience.

Also on this playing field are those who see the inner spiritual life as synonymous with their outer works and efforts. They see little difference between the outer and the inner life. They have a long list of the things that they do for or with God. (Bible reading and prayer being two of them.) Armed with this list of good works, they are convinced that they walk with God because of all of the things that they are doing for Him. Unfortunately, their frantic pace to keep God "pleased" and their conscience satisfied does not allow them to *"be still and know that I am God." (Psalm 46:10)*

Somewhere along the way, all three of these groups got away from what God intended and fortified themselves, each within their own cardboard box of tradition and practice. They each are sincere. They each have good and helpful points to make. However, if we are going to understand walking with God, we are going to have to go back in time to a place before the box. That place is the Tabernacle of the Old Testament.

The Bible says that our body is the temple of the Holy Ghost. *(First Corinthians 6:19)* God no longer lives in the Tabernacle of Moses or the Temple of Solomon, but instead, He chooses to reside in the hearts of believers themselves. Because of this, there are some parallels that we can draw from those old places of worship concerning our devotional life and extending to a lifestyle of worship.

Let's talk about what we often call the believer's "devotions" or "quiet time". In short, there needs to be a time set aside each day for you to get alone with God and talk with

Him just as Adam and Eve did in the Garden of Eden. How a vibrant inner spiritual life looks varies depending upon your personality, emotional makeup, and the family/living situation in which you find yourself. This is something that has been neglected by the "fit into our box" approach that has been advocated over the years.

God is the God of the individual, and as such, He relates to us as individuals. That fact then, impacts our individual practice of what we call our devotional life.

Some people have been known to lock themselves in a room to talk to God alone; others sit on a log in the woods reading the Scriptures; while others in our modern day shut out the world with their headphones and read the words of God on their Ipad while sitting in Starbucks. There is no formula; no set way of doing things. God is the God of the individual. Because of this, we each approach Him in our own individual way but through the same means. (The Bible, study, prayer, meditation, praise, worship, etc...) Here are some thoughts concerning the tabernacle/temple and our private time with God.

The Role of Silence *(Habakkuk 2:20, Ecclesiastes 3:7)* – Here we aren't saying that we must be silent during our daily time with God. The point is that here wasn't anything inside the Holy Place or Holy of Holies designed to make noise and distract. If we are going to spend quality time with God, we have to make the decision that we are going to shut out distractions. For couples with children, that means some negotiation as to who is going to referee fights and repair skinned knees at what times, but make sure your spouse has quiet time alone with God.

The Role of Solitude *(Matthew 14:23, Hebrews 9:7)* - You can be alone in a crowded room, I'll give you that. But as for me, a quiet corner of the house or sitting near a country stream is a whole lot better than trying to ignore everyone else. God is a jealous God. He wants time with just you because He wants you to know Him on a deep level. We wouldn't treat our relationship with our spouse the way we at times treat God and our quiet time. Undivided attention...it's what He deserves, and the only way to get close to Him in an intimate and undistracted way.

The Role of Music *(First Chronicles 6:32; 9:33-34; 16:4-6)* - I know that I have just broken my own rule about silence. But if we look at the temple, they had musicians. Whether you sing to God in praise or turn on worshipful music and meditate on the words sung by others, music has the ability to move our emotions in the direction of our Creator. Don't neglect music. It is a very useful emotional tool and emotion is a part of worship.

The Role of Food *(Numbers 4:7, Exodus 40:23)* - Remember the table of Shewbread? Let's make two applications here:

First, we know that the Bible refers to itself as the "milk" and the "meat". *(Hebrews 5:12)* We cannot properly build that inner relationship without reading (or listening) to the Scriptures as part of our devotions. To neglect the Bible is to have a one-way conversation with God.

Second, there is an application concerning our physical food. If our body is the temple of God, we should be more careful concerning our diet. *(First Corinthians 10:31)* Many times we do not have the energy to get up early or stay up late to talk to God because we have fed our bodies junk throughout the day.

The Role of Light *(Exodus 25:31; 35:14)* - It is

interesting to note that the only light in the Holy Place came from the lampstand. God could have lit up the whole place as bright as high noon in the Sahara, but He didn't. I'm not much of a candle person myself, but I do know that there is a certain mood derived from candles and softer lighting features (like a reading lamp) These lighting fixtures can help set an atmosphere that is more relaxing and for most people, more conducive to reflection and contemplation.

The Role of Sacrifice *(Exodus 20:24; Romans 12:1-2)* - Let's be real here. Building an inner relationship with God takes sacrifice. There are some things that you will have to give up to achieve what you want to in this area. Whether it is sin that has to be confessed and forsaken, food that is left untouched during a fasting time, or time that has to be reallocated; sacrifices must be made.

The Role of Washing *(Exodus 30:18)* - The laver, or basin, was a large bowl filled with water located halfway between the brazen altar and the Holy Place. It was there the priests washed the daily grime off their hands and feet. As we walk through this world, we have the dirt of our lives that has to be confessed and forsaken. Don't go through your time with God feeling dirty; get washed first. *(Ephesians 5:26, First John 1:9)*

The Role of Prayer *(I Samuel 1:17, Luke 2:37, Romans 12:12, Philippians 4:6)* - I'm not going to try to replicate great writing that has already been done on this topic. Get a copy of any of the following. Each expresses a different aspect of the prayer life and all have been helpful to believers over the years.

- Any of E.M. Bounds'[7] books on prayer
- *Rees Howells: Intercessor* by Norman Percy Grubb[8]
- *Praying Backwards* by Bryan Chappell[12]
- *Asking and Receiving* by John R. Rice[13]

These are great resources in teaching and inspiring us to pray.

As for me, to start with, I generally work my way through the parts of the Lord's Prayer and make each statement my own. Then I try to ask the Holy Spirit what He wants me to pray for that day. I just figure that He will urge me to pray for those things that are on His heart. God will bring to mind and urge us to pray the prayers to which He desires to give answers. *(Romans 8:26)*

The Role of Fasting *(Nehemiah 9:1, Daniel 9:3, Matthew 9:15)* - The Jews had several national fasts in the year. This is a bigger topic than we have space for in this chapter. Just take note that showing God you are serious by giving up something that is important to you is no small thing in His eyes.

The Role of Time *(Ephesians 5:16, Colossians 4:5, Exodus 23:15 "the time appointed")* - May I urge you to think about doing life slower? What are you trying to accomplish at breakneck speed anyway? Do you see Jesus acting like that? He was here to save the world but never looked like He was in a rush. Oh, we have responsibilities and cannot spend untold hours in silence before Him. But averaged out, we ought to be able to say that we have spent significant and quality time with God. Understand that time with God does not require us to be alone with Him in a room for hours on end, but does require us to be in a mindset where we are communicating with Him and open to His direction as we walk through our day. That is what He desires.

The Role of Sanctification *(Exodus 13:12, Psalm 4:3, Leviticus 20:7, First Peter 3:15)* - At its most basic, the word "sanctification" means to be set apart from all else and to be dedicated wholly to God. That level of dedication is missing in our Christianity today. We have many fickle Christians that bounce from church to church, book to book, and teacher to teacher with no real sense that they are supposed to be building line upon line and precept upon precept. *(Isaiah 8:10)* Commitment is key. The temple was set apart for God. The Levites were dedicated to the service of God. If you are going to be successful in your inner relationship with God, you are going to have to be committed to God.

The Role of Centrality *(Deuteronomy 23:14, Numbers 2:2)* - The tabernacle was set in the middle of the Jewish encampment. It was central to their lives. The question then is whether or not your relationship with God is central to your life or a convenient addition. Is your relationship only that fifteen minutes in the morning, or do you have an ongoing conversation with Him throughout the day? Is He central?

The Role of the Supremacy of the Cross of Jesus *(Colossians 2:17, Hebrews 10:1)* - The tabernacle and the temple were completely soaked through with symbols of Jesus and His work on the cross. Be careful in your devotional life that you don't become the focus. With quiet time, it is easy to become introspective instead of *"looking unto Jesus"* as the Scriptures command. *(Hebrews 12:2)*

The Role of Repetition *(Hebrews 10:11)* - Here is where we have to hit a balance. The activity of the temple was very much an activity of repetition. We like repetition; especially, as we get older. However, don't get so ingrained with your repetition that it becomes empty tradition or worse. *(Matthew 6:7; Mark 7:13)* We must follow the Holy Spirit in our quiet time. Sometimes He will allow us to be comfortable in repetition; at other times, His quiet voice urges us to change up our routine.

The Role of Beauty *(Psalm 27:4, Exodus 28:2, First*

Chronicles 16:29, Second Chronicles 3:6) - This is a lesser detail, but its truth cannot be denied. The tabernacle and temple had aspects of great beauty.

Let's make two applications. First, sometimes it is helpful and healthy to talk with God in places of beauty like a summer field or a park bench along the seashore. Second, we must view our relationship with God as a thing of beauty that both we and God are working on together.

The Role of Death *(Genesis 22:13, Hebrews 10:3-4, Exodus 29)* - When we view the tabernacle, we cannot get away from the fact of death. Of course, the death of bulls and goats pictured the coming death of Jesus, our final sacrifice. Let us not forget, however, that the Bible says that when Jesus died, we died with Him and rose as new creatures in Christ. *(Romans 6-8)* If we accept as fact our death to sin and our resurrection to love and serve God, it will put us in the right frame of mind for our walk with God.

The Role of Praise *(First Chronicles 16:8-10, 23-25)* - David talked about entering *"his courts with praise"*. *(Psalm 100:4)* Let's not be selfish worshippers; coming to God with our list of demands like He is some kind of cosmic genie. We need to praise the King of the Universe not because we get anything, but because He is who He is.

I'm sure there are other parallels that we could draw from the tabernacle and temple, but that will suffice for now. Below are some random thoughts in regard to building our inner relationship.

- Be faithful during the dry spells. The inner life is not always exhilarating. God does not allow us to stay permanently on the mountain tops. Dry spells teach us determination and surrender.

- Guard your time with God.
- Seek to understand the depth of God's love for you and rest in it.
- Seek God...not the gifts that He gives.
- Reject thoughts that distract or undermine your faith.
- Paul said...'that I may know Him' (Phil 3:10)
- Renounce whatever does not lead you closer to God.
- Understand that we come to God upon the basis of the merits of Christ. It has nothing to do with our own goodness or works. We can only do good because of Christ in us.
- Our motivation needs to come from the love of God for us and the will of God for our lives. We cannot be motivated by the goal of gaining comfort for our own problems from God.
- God won't allow a searching soul to be comforted anywhere but with Him.
- To be with Him, we must cultivate the habit of thinking of Him often. - God is there. It is rude to leave a visiting friend alone.
- Give God control of your 'stuff'. "*where your treasure is, there will your heart be also.*"*(Matt.6:21)*
- Accept His forgiveness, cleansing, and unqualified love for you.
- See yourself as God sees you...not as a criminal to be judged, but as a son to be loved, trained, and corrected.
- God never leaves us, but sometimes He hides His face from us. It is at this time that He shows us our need of Him and tests our commitment to Him.

One last thought:

A few weeks ago one of my sisters asked my father the question. "How did people two hundred years ago who did not have a personal copy of the Bible have devotions?" I think that is a valid question. Here was his answer. "They learned and memorized the Bible and had a devotional walk with God throughout not a 20 minute warm up for the day."

If we are going to get back to a time before pre-manufactured Christianity (the box), we are going to have to be authentic, unique, consistent, individual, and intimate in our walk with God.

3. SUCCESS BEFORE THE BOX

I was sitting in church one day, and a well-known university president who was speaking that day made this statement, "The greatest preacher on this earth is known only to his tribe or village."

Up to this point I understood the idea of faithfulness, but I faultily assumed that faithfulness combined with the right ministry formula guaranteed measurable success in ministry.

For good or bad, we are all the product of the decades and centuries of history that took place before our birth. This is true especially in the church because of the church's heavy reliance upon tradition. It is essential therefore, for each generation to Biblically examine what has been brought forward by default from the past and either approve or discard it.

Getting back to church success; somewhere in the middle of the last century, the power of God got replaced in many church programs with the power of promotion. Slick advertising and splashy incentives (prizes/rewards) pushed the idea that success was size and numbers. Even today, more than a half century later we find that churches and church leaders are still using the measurements of attendance, baptisms, and offering to evaluate one another.

We must stop here and remind ourselves of **Second Corinthians 10:12, "For we dare not make ourselves of the number, or compare ourselves with some that commend themselves: but they measuring themselves by themselves, and comparing themselves among themselves, are not wise."**

It just doesn't make sense to compare the city church with the country church; to compare the aged church with the church plant; to compare the mission outpost with the mega church. When we do so, we find ourselves either looking down upon a brother and feeding our pride, or looking down upon ourselves and feeding self-pity. Either way, it harms us spiritually and is sinful.

Since Henry Ford's assembly line built the automobile, success has been defined by how many widgets your company can make and how much money you made. So what was success before it got taken over by the modern era?

The rise of the middle class in North America and Europe over the past hundred years has fueled a high octane mixture of drive and ambition to rise to the top. We call it "climbing the corporate ladder". Unfortunately, this vulgar ambition has seeped into the church in such a way that we don't even know (or apparently care) what God considers to be "success" anymore.

In my mind, the preeminent verse regarding success in the Bible is in **Joshua 1:8**. It says, **"This book of the law shall not depart out of thy mouth; but thou shalt meditate therein day and night, that thou mayest observe to do** *according to all that is written therein: for then thou shalt make thy way prosperous, and then thou shalt have good success."*

Simply put, our success is evaluated on the basis of our obedience to the Bible. So then, our churches are operating off of the wrong metrics. Instead of measuring attendance, baptisms, and money, we should be looking at setting goals of obedience like:

- How many people have taken a forward step in their Christian life this week?
- How many people have we witnessed to for Jesus this week?
- How many physical needs did we meet this week?
- How many hours have we spent visiting with outsiders to cultivate relationships for Jesus?
- How many people are we discipling?
- How many volunteer hours have we invested in others? (Jesus came to *"minister and to give his life a ransom for many" – Matthew 20:28*. We remember the "give my life" part, but we forget to emulate the "minister" part.)
- How many prayer requests from people outside the faith are on our list? (If they trust you with a prayer request {prayer is spiritual}, it is an open door to talk about the spiritual with them.)

Measuring our obedience is much more useful than measuring results that we cannot control. Having said this, a caution is necessary. We must always be careful that we are not making good goals into expectations and the rule by which we judge one another. That would be wrong.

What we have done successfully at Northside is that from time to time we will take six or eight weeks and keep track of these statistics of obedience. To do this, we use a blind survey card at offering time combined with a blind electronic survey. In this way, we encourage people to be intentional in their obedience without embarrassing people or setting up a judgment structure. By using a blind survey and a limited time frame we avoid the trouble caused when measurements get institutionalized and turned into arbitrary rules by which Christians judge one another. The people of Northside have enjoyed this encouragement of obedience. Each week of the experiment serves as a reminder and we see the corporate numbers go up as the individuals in the congregation catch on to the concept of intentionally following Christ daily in these areas.

But let's get back to talking about Jesus…

What were things like before the box? Jesus couldn't have been considered a success. He had twelve guys, one was a traitor, and only one of the other eleven showed up at His execution.

Paul and the rest of the apostles journeyed through the dust of the known world with little or no money, meeting with ten believers here and fifty there. After this, they had the pain of a martyr's death. This is not exactly great material for a recruitment poster.

Formulating a real God-oriented view of success requires that we look at some of the faithful prophets and realize that Jeremiah came by the "weeping prophet" name by witnessing nothing but the moral decline and ultimate failure his nation. Perhaps we may be headed into a similar experience, and yet we must remain faithful to the Lord. God's timing for the measurement of success is the issue we must grapple with. Our success will not be properly measured until the Judgment Seat *(Second Corinthians 5:10)* and the assignments given to us in the Millennial Kingdom Age *(Revelation 5:9-10; 20:6)*. At present, we should be equipping God's people for failure and faithfulness, but that does not make a popular motivational speech. Everyone wants "success" as seen through the eyes of our current culture. Everyone wants their fifteen minutes of fame and acclaim, but that wasn't the experience of most of the prophets and preachers of the Bible.

God has a master plan that is not going to fail. Ultimately, I want to play my part in that plan, even if it means living in the shadow and humiliation of (what at this time appears to be) human failure.

Unfortunately, the few big names and huge crowds of the great revivals of the past have given modern Christians the idea that God isn't happy and that God isn't working if you don't have this type of "success".

We have to remember that history has evidenced cycles of revival, plateau, and decline. The pastor and church that labour faithfully in a society of declining spiritual interest are just as successful in the eyes of God as those fortunate pastors and churches in history who were present at a time when, in God's providence, society turned back to God in a wave.

Let's think about Noah and his ark. He preached for years without converts outside of his family. We hold the great missionaries of the past in high esteem. Several of the notable missionaries went years without seeing converts, and yet in North America we look down upon and privately criticize churches because we don't see our version of "success" played out in their lives.

Dr. Bob Jones Sr.[9], Methodist Evangelist and founder of Bob Jones University said, "Real success is knowing the will of God and doing it". Anything short of that, and you have failed. However, if you know and do the will of God, people can apply whatever measuring stick they want to your church and ministry, and you can rest comfortably knowing that God sees you as a success. And in the end, that's all that really matters.

So, what was success before the box of modern "success"? Success was knowing the will of God and doing it. That's all.

4. PROGRAMS BEFORE THE BOX

"We have to have it. All the other churches do!" I remember the first time I heard this tired old line. I was standing in front of the church moderating a business meeting. An older gentleman was instructing the congregation on how we just have to have a Sunday School and a youth group. Now, I have nothing particularly against either of these programs. The problem was, at that time in our small church the only little girl we had for Sunday School was the daughter of our Sunday School teacher. It didn't make sense for mom and girl to come to the church building an hour early for something that could be (and should be) taught at home through the week. At that time, we had two teens old enough for youth group. Neither had any friends to invite, and they didn't get along with each other! When we "have to have" certain programs, it would be wise to ask, "Why?"

The other old nugget I have heard over the years when presenting a new idea has been, "Do any of the other (place your brand of church here) churches do it?" This question assumes that if our particular bunch of churches have a particular program or idea, then it must be okay. Inversely it says that if an idea comes from outside our little circle, then it must be wrong. The last thing the question intimates is that if no other church, inside or outside our circle, is enacting this idea, we don't want to be the first to try it. It might be heretical. Or worse in some congregations eyes, it might not work!

The truth is that programs come and go. Sunday School is relatively new in the two thousand plus years of church history. Before this, parents actually took their job of training their children in the Bible at home seriously. Youth groups led by paid youth pastors is an even more recent phenomenon than Sunday School is.

The problem is that over the years a program template (let's call it what it is…a box) has developed and your church is considered odd or maybe even heretical if you don't have all of the prerequisite programs. Worse yet, if a church begins a program that isn't already in the template, charges of compromise and caving into a "sinful culture of change" come all too quickly.

But what about before the box? When we look at Scripture we find that programs were very few. The most notable program was the establishment of a group of seven men to make sure the widows were fed and cared for. (**Acts 6**)

The early church, however, did have processes. Evangelism had a process. It was go, baptize, and teach. There was a process for church discipline and a process for collecting money to help the troubled church at Jerusalem. There was a process for the religious education of children: parents!

In my opinion, processes are superior to programs. Processes seem to be more people oriented. They can be grasped more readily and people understand immediately what is being asked of them. Programs seem to be institutional in emphasis and tend to take on a life of their own. Even after a program has outlived its effectiveness, churches are hesitant to suspend it for fear that it may be a sign of spiritual weakness or that they will be labeled "quitters."

Many individuals can take personal responsibility for, ownership of, and involvement in a process. Only a few get to do the same in a program. The challenge is that processes are harder to define and difficult to manage in a top-down structure. Also, helping people through a process rather than plugging them into a program takes more hands on effort.

Processes are a very individualized thing because they are individualized in their pace. There are some who fly through a process, and others who methodically crawl along. We live in an Ipod generation. (Remember when we all gathered around the record player or the boom box? Community has been traded for individualism. Whether that is good or bad is irrelevant to our discussion. It is today's culture, and we have to minister to people who know nothing else.) In the end, having a process for new believers, new church members, children, youth, etc. may be more beneficial in relating to this new mindset.

Of course, I am not saying that programs are bad. I am only arguing that they must produce results. By results, I do not mean an increase in attendance or an uptick in the program's financial aspect. What I do mean is that every program must have a clearly defined set of spiritual goals, and every program must be held to the standard of those goals in a regular evaluation process. We must not have programs for the sake of having programs.

The programs that we do have must fit the unique community situation and the giftings of the people within that particular church. For example, a church with medical doctors in it has a program through which those in the medical field meet the physical needs of those in a third world nation. A little church in farm country shouldn't feel that they have to have that particular ministry. They would be far more effective finding their niche in their community to represent Jesus well.

Whether it is a program or a process we must not allow any particular ministry facet to escape regular and serious review to ensure that it is gospel driven, Biblically sound, culturally relevant, and still achieving its stated goals.

Let's take a few minutes together and talk about how a process differs from a program. The average church's programs consist of church services, Sunday School, youth group, visitation of the sick, evangelization efforts, etc... These are not bad things. They are good things. In fact, programs can be a part of an effective process in the church. However, the challenge with programs is that very often those people in our churches (and sometimes the leadership) do not know and have not thought through how all of these diverse programs work together in helping someone make progress in their spiritual life. We assume that because we have always had these and other stock programs, that they must work seamlessly together to accomplish one goal: Christian maturity. Many times that is not the case.

A process shows the interrelation between the programs. In a church that runs programs and does well with them, there is a process that is running in the background keeping those programs in sync with each other and with the ultimate purposes of the church.

Andy Stanley[14], pastor of North Point Church in the Atlanta area says that if we are trying to implement processes we need to learn to "think in steps." You see, a process is what happens in a car assembly plant. There, the car begins as a rolling chassis and goes from station to station having various parts put onto it. Eventually, it rolls out of the assembly plant and onto the truck that takes it to the dealers and the showroom floor. Each stop along the way in this assembly process has been designed with the final goal in sight: A Brand New Car! (Applause here please.)

A program is different. A program doesn't see the big picture or the final goal. That is why there are so many turf wars among the different program departments in a church. Each individual department doesn't realize that they are only one stop along the assembly line. They don't see that a process is running (or should be) in the background interlocking all of the programs of a church. Once people are made aware of the process and their place in it, cooperation comes easier.

Whether you are conscious of it or not, your church has a process. Likely it is a process that is based on tradition. You see, a process speaks to how and why we do things. In most churches the how and why is answered by, "That's how we've always done it." That is bad process management.

It is thinking through the process that allows us to put in place the steps necessary for us to contact someone; get them to understand the Gospel and trust Christ; come through the door of the building; be baptized and mentored; get into a church service; into a Bible study group; then into a ministry where they can serve. This is all one big process. It is many stops along the railway line heading toward a final destination. That's what makes it a process!

Have you thought through the "flow chart" of your ministry? Everyone that comes to your church is at a different stage in their Christian life. If you haven't thought through the process and found a simple way to communicate and explain that process to them, how do they know where to fit? Because of this lack of understanding of process many believers find themselves sitting and waiting for years for someone to tell them where they fit and where to get involved; still others dive in (or are pulled in by well-meaning but misguided folks) and soon find that they are in the deep end of the pool when they should have started nearer to the beginning of the process. Simply put, if there is not a process, and if it is not simply explained, you can bet that there will be spiritual casualties.

A few years ago Thom Rainer[15] and Eric Geiger[16] did a lot of research and surveys that culminated in the publication of a book called *"Simple Church: Returning to God's Process for Making Disciples."* Although we cannot determine the will of God and the direction of the church by means of surveys, their conclusions were interesting. They determined that those churches that did the best at attracting and holding on to people were those that had simple, well explained processes.

We need to think through the steps that are necessary to have in place in order to connect with people, talk to them about Jesus, baptize them, and mentor them. We need to think through the steps we need to put in place regarding the saved individual who is coming into our church for the first time. Where do they fit? How do they know? What are the next steps for them? How does one go from casually attending, to becoming a member of the church, to growing in grace, to serving in a ministry area? All along the way there are little steps that make up that process. If a step is missing or crooked, no one wants to climb the staircase. Too many churches leave people bottlenecked at the bottom of the stairs because they have not thought through the process of climbing the stairs. This results in immature believers, and it is not entirely their fault.

Processes, unlike programs, can be learned, mastered, and replicated by the individual. Processes have benchmarks that show what progress one has made and a goal/destination to show where one must go. Programs only have the ability to measure numbers of quantity. (how many people, how much money) Processes have measurements of progress and quality, and quality is always better than quantity.

Simple processes lessen communication breakdowns in the church. If the process is communicated well, everyone knows what is going on. Informed people are happy people! If a process has been well-thought-out it will have a predictable result. Plug and play programs are not so predictable.

So, I have had to get out my pen and paper and put together my steps into flow charts. From there I have had to find simple and effective ways of communicating not only what we are doing; but how and why.

Having said all of this, I am not down on programs. Programs are good! However, we must pair them down to those that are effective steps along the way in the process. Nothing must escape scrutiny and evaluation. In this way, we make the program part of a means to reach the goal and not an end in and of itself.

It is true that the North American church is over-programmed and that most churches have accepted tradition (the default process) instead of thinking through and implementing an effective process. Therefore, the only responsible thing for us to do is to climb out of the over-programmed box of today to see what God has for our particular church. This is the only way we can, as a unique congregation, impact our unique community with the gospel of Jesus.

5. CONSISTENCY AND BALANCE BEFORE THE BOX

Consistency and balance are the hardest things of the Christian life. There is nothing more challenging for us personally or corporately. Stating emphatically that we are consistent and balanced is kind of like shouting from the rooftop that we are humble. If we have to say it, we probably aren't. Having said that, it is my contention that we can do much better in the areas of consistency and balance.

Consistency and balance problems are not new issues. For most of us (regardless of our affiliation or tribe), the box that we find ourselves in is rusted with the holes of inconsistency and imbalance because of church and denominational insistence upon certain traditions, methods, and practices that are not spelled out in the Bible.

Let's talk for a moment about the difference between consistency and faithfulness. We are consistent when our doctrine impacts our lives in such a way that each aspect of our life and ministry is aligned with the purposes and plan of God. Inconsistency springs from the addition of man's ideas, traditions, and expectations into that mix.

Faithfulness, however, is a different ballgame. Faithfulness gives to us more of a connotation of loyalty and fidelity to a specific thing, person, or idea. Many times, folks are faithful to their doctrinal and practical positions because of a fidelity toward a man, a group of churches, or a denominational church structure. This of course, is a problem. It puts people into what I refer to as a "state of consistent inconsistency". If we allow our fidelity to others to cultivate a stand that is not Biblically balanced, we are inconsistent no matter how faithful we are to that stand. Our faithfulness needs to be pinned to Jesus and to a plain, contextual interpretation and application of His Scriptures. Anything else only encloses us in a box of inconsistency that is made by man.

When the Bible gives us instruction, it is both consistent and balanced. But when we take it upon ourselves to add to (or read into) Scripture our own version of traditions, methods, and practices; at the very least, we set ourselves up for accusations of hypocrisy. The danger, of course, is that our Christianity becomes so entangled with these extra-Biblical additions that it does not survive when our inconsistency and imbalance are exposed.

Consistency and balance have always been a problem. It seems though that these challenges have become more pronounced with the continual fractionalization of the churches. As each group of believers retreats to their corner and defends it, certain truths are emphasized, and others neglected, negated, or eliminated in order to affirm the position which that particular group espouses. In order to say that "we are better," and in order to clearly differentiate ourselves from others, we have created a scenario of inconsistency and imbalance that becomes our box.

Consistency, of course, does not mean that we are now what we have always been. That position leaves no room for the direction of the Holy Spirit or spiritual growth. Consistency in the Christian life has much more to do with direction than it does with position. Some would argue, "I am consistent because I have the same stand on everything as I did forty years ago." This does not prove consistency as much as it does stagnation. God demands growth.

First Peter 2:2 As newborn babes, desire the sincere milk of the word, that ye may grow thereby:

Second Peter 3:18 But grow in grace, and in the knowledge of our Lord and Saviour Jesus Christ. To him be glory both now and for ever. Amen.

Growth is change, and change in the right direction is a good thing and can be correctly deemed "consistent." The right direction of course, is nearer the Bible and Jesus Christ.

It is evident in all the various camps of Christianity that Biblical consistency has been sidelined by the scramble to establish simple answers to complex questions in order to gain a following. People want the easy answer; the quick fix. This is part of the problem. There are no easy and simple answers to life's challenges. Life is messy, and so, the answers are necessarily intricate and nuanced.

If we have learned anything from politics, we have learned that in general, people do not want to think for themselves. They want pat answers spoon fed to them in innovative and entertaining ways. We live in a soundbite generation. On both ends of the Christian spectrum, we find people living on the soundbites and platitudes of their favourite preacher or teacher, and parts of verses wrenched out of context.

Just look at what I lovingly (well maybe not) call the "Christian Knick-Knack Industry." If there is a Bible verse (or part of one) that sounds inspiring or comforting, it is torn from its context and slapped on a mug, a trophy, or a t-shirt. Worse still, are the common sayings that people honestly think are Scripture, and they ignorantly base life decisions on them.

This approach to Christianity has produced shallow, immature, inconsistent Christians who are reliant upon that preacher or teacher who is delivering their "quote of the day." This does great damage to the individual Christian's responsibility to study the Bible for themselves as found in **Second Timothy 2:15**. In addition, this does harm to the concept of the priesthood of the believer and our individual responsibility to check out what the preacher/teacher says and to make an informed decision concerning the truth or error of it.

Acts 17:11 These were more noble than those in Thessalonica, in that they received the word with all readiness of mind, and searched the scriptures daily, whether those things were so.

If we are just accepting pat answers, then we are not adhering to the spirit of the above verses. In addition, it is just misguided to think that the complex issues of life can be summed up in a sentence or two with no nuance or application to the specific situation in which we find ourselves.

Involved in all of this is the strong tendency to use consistency as an excuse to justify inconsistent beliefs, practices, and traditions. Just because we have always done something in one way does not make us consistent. In fact, our insistence upon a particular thing based solely upon tradition may put us in the place of inconsistency.

Two plus two always equals four. We run into trouble with our consistency when we allow in one aspect of our personal life or public ministry what we won't allow in another. For example (and this is where I get in trouble with the preachers), most pastors have massive libraries either in book or electronic form.

Those libraries (and I have yet to find an exception) are inconsistent. Dozens of divergent beliefs and doctrinal positions are represented, many of which that pastor would not endorse, and yet he will glean what he can (in a Biblically framed conscience) agree with and ignore what he cannot accept.

I am not saying that this approach to a library is wrong (It describes well my library.) but if a _____(place denomination here) writer is good enough to read, sift through, and glean from, but we wouldn't sit down, talk with, and befriend him because we differ on some things; then we are inconsistent. Some excuse their libraries by saying that that writer is dead and wrote long ago. So then the logical, consistent conclusion becomes, "Differing opinions are okay and are useful to me as long as the fellow I differ with is dead."

Another popular rationalization for utilizing materials from dead men of another denomination has been, "Things were different then." Well they were, and they weren't. It is true that there wasn't as much conflict amongst church leaders in secondary areas like music, methods, church models, and Bible translations. (Note: there were times in the past when there were disputes over the introduction of new translations as well.) However, there was at that time, as is now, a diversity of doctrinal positions. To justify our use of these materials upon the basis of "things were different then" ignores this fact.

At this point, a disclaimer is in order. There are men that we can fellowship with, and even learn from on a personal basis, but because of their divergent beliefs on some points of doctrine we cannot endorse them and confuse young believers within our congregations by asking them to speak at our churches.

Having said that; if it is necessary to have 100% agreement with a guest speaker in order to have him in our churches, then we will have a very small group of men from which to choose. In addition, our congregations will miss out on men with training in specialized areas (like finance, addictions, creation science, or parenting) because they do not line up in every secondary issue unrelated to their specialty.

Consistency is one of those things that I respect. There are those who live very consistent, extremely cloistered lives shutting out every facet of the modern world. I can respect that even though that is not my choice. On the other hand, I can respect the man that discerningly and Biblically sifts through what modern society has to offer and chooses what he in a Biblically-framed good conscience can be involved in. Both are consistent positions, but when these positions are mixed then there is room for the accusation of hypocrisy.

Consistency is an all or nothing thing. If we are not consistent in an area, we have to admit to ourselves and those that follow us that we are inconsistent and pragmatic in that area. Pragmatism for consistency's sake, although not wrong in and of itself, can become a problem because it makes an otherwise consistent stand difficult to defend. Inconsistencies are the hooks that we eventually get hanged upon.

Lady justice is blind. In one hand, she holds a sword, in the other hand a balance scale. It is unfortunate, but I have seen too many well- meaning Christians swing the sword without looking toward the scale of balance. This, in turn, has hurt families, divided churches, and destroyed lives.

The Bible is not an easy book. If it was, I would have figured it all out years ago, as would have you. The reason we have so many solid, well-meaning Christians with divergent views on secondary issues (which I roughly define as those not relating directly to and impacting on the function of the gospel) is that we each emphasize one area of Scripture or another, often depending upon the circumstance in which we find ourselves. For example, the happy man will read the Psalms and see the lighter side of David as he lifts his song in praise. The man depressed will read the same Psalms and identify with a lonely David who ran for his life and sought a God who seemed to be absent at times.

We find in the Bible what we are looking for, and that is good. But we must also force ourselves to see the other side of the equation. An imbalance in the physical body means sickness, and it is no different spiritually. To overemphasize one truth to the detriment of another will cause spiritual imbalance and disease.

For example, stereotypically there is a denomination that heavily over-emphasizes the work of the Holy Spirit to the risk of ignoring other important aspects of Biblical truth. On the other end of the spectrum are those other denominations in which you rarely hear His name mentioned. Neither of these positions are healthy. The Holy Spirit is a real person whom Jesus sent to be with us until He (Jesus) comes back. To ignore the Spirit is dismal failure; to have an imbalanced focus upon the Spirit to the potential abandonment of other truth is equally dismal.

Another example of imbalance is the ever popular debate

regarding the sovereignty of God versus the free will of man in salvation. The parameters of this book do not allow for a full discussion of this topic but suffice it to say that the Bible balances sovereignty and free will. Careful study will bear this out. Those who ignore that balance to prove their point and their own perceived spiritual superiority do so at their own peril.

Whether it is in the pulpit or in the home, balance must be held as a high virtue. Many I have talked to will overemphasize the love of God almost to the dismissal of all of His other attributes. Something is wrong there. On the other hand, there are those who will not strongly speak of a God of love for fear of being labeled as being soft on sin.

There is a balance. It is found in the Bible, but we have to seriously study the Word of God. Imbalance is usually the first sign of an immature or alternatively, a lazy Christian.

Unfortunately, if this same immaturity is evidenced in local church leadership then a whole congregation can be thrown into imbalance. This is a tragedy.

Today, in every tradition and denomination of Christianity, we find evidence of imbalance and inconsistency. It is a troubling part of the boxes that we have created for ourselves. However, through careful study of the Word of God and a conscientious examination and reinvention of our traditions, methods, practices, and teachings, we can live the balanced and consistent lives that we should.

6. MISSIONS AND WORLD EVANGELISM BEFORE THE BOX

In this century, most of missions has been relegated to the local church supporting either para-church ministries directly or supporting individual missionaries through a para-church organization.

While Biblically there is no direct problem with a para-church support agency (commonly called a mission board), it should be noted that this box that we are presently in was not here originally. In the New Testament, we find the Holy Spirit sending individuals out of an individual local church.

Acts 13:2 As they ministered to the Lord, and fasted, the Holy Ghost said, Separate me Barnabas and Saul for the work whereunto I have called them.

The point of the supremacy of the local church has been made loudly and effectively, and denominations that seek heavy-handed control of the local congregation are in decline. However, in the area of missions, too many times the local church has been pushed into the role of "give and pray." Accountability for and care of the individual missionary has

49

been outsourced to the missions agency. This is the box that we currently occupy.

This is not to say that cooperation is not needed. If we look at the New Testament, we find that the apostle Paul encouraged a number of churches to help with the needs of the persecuted church in Jerusalem. *(Romans 15:25-26)*

Cooperation, most times is hindered by men of good intentions with an over emphasis on small details. Pastors and groups of churches with good hearts allow differences of opinion and application of Scripture (as opposed to interpretation) to sidetrack the effort of working together in world evangelism. The message of the gospel then gets sidetracked or lost because of a stormy sea of personalities and personal preferences that have morphed into corporate convictions and rules.

In the New Testament, we find a lot of different churches at a number of different development stages. Also, we have churches struggling with serious moral and doctrinal issues. Strangely enough, the apostle Paul chose to work through those issues with them rather than disassociating himself. Having said this, there is a time to walk away from cooperation and fellowship. But this should be a last-resort step. It should be over an issue that impacts the fabric of the Christian faith, the core of the Gospel.

In regard to the missionaries themselves, the box that we now find ourselves in is a very odd model indeed. Basically the idea is that we send from our church a husband and wife "team" of missionaries out on their own with their children in tow to a life of isolation on the mission field. It is no wonder that we have fewer people going into full time missions, and fewer still staying at it past a few terms on the field.

Before the box, things were different. The story of the book of Acts shows us first that the method for missions is team ministry. Paul did not go out alone; neither did Barnabas later on. They travelled and ministered as a team. Secondly, we discover that the Holy Spirit sent out teams of men.

That doesn't mean that ladies don't and shouldn't have a role to play in missions. The Bible shows us that they do. However, let's be fair to the missionary's wife. She has had to leave her family, friends, and security. She has been brought into a new country, culture and language; most times with several children in her care. Many times, because of the condition of local public school (or lack thereof) she has to homeschool her children or face the guilt of sending them to boarding school. She doesn't have the time or energy to be her husband's "team" in evangelism and church building. She often has all she can handle being the "home team."

God intended for a team of individuals (missionary pastors and support workers) to join together for a common cause in one geographical area. This is different than dropping a "missionary couple" with their little children in Sudan and saying, "Go tell them about Jesus." This sounds heartless because it is, but that is what we do. Just because this was the way it was done in the past, doesn't mean it is the best way or the Biblical way.

The problem is stubborn, hard-headed preachers back home in North America that are clueless in regard to the realities on the ground in missions both at home (church planting) and abroad (foreign missions). This makes them look very heartless to their missionaries. I've heard men say, "Well, we already have a missionary there in _____ (fill in the mission field.) We can't support you to go there as well." With that kind of unBiblical drivel passing for reasoning, Paul and his entourage (we spell that TEAM) would never have gotten financial backing to shake their known world with the gospel.

Another problem with our world evangelism box today is the thought that the missionary needs to be the one to keep us (the supporting church) informed, and thus encouraged to continue praying for and sending money to him. We get this idea from a faulty reading of Paul's epistles. For some reason, we think that Paul was writing back to his supporting churches to let them know what was going on.

Does any real study of the Bible back that up? The answer is, "No." Paul was the founder of most of the churches to which he wrote. He was the spiritual father helping, instructing, correcting, and encouraging his little missions churches. Yes, these little church plants helped Paul out financially from time to time but reporting back to them was not the reason for his letters. In our modern context Paul would have been more like the home church pastor than the missionary out there reporting back.

To be fair, Paul did tell the church at Antioch what had happened on their missionary journey. *(Acts 14:26, 27)* The rest of the story is that this was their "home /sending church", and they weren't away all that long. This is akin to a group taking a month on a short-term missions trip and showing their pictures when they get home. This was not a whole bunch of local churches demanding to be encouraged and informed by their missionary every month. Give your missionary trust and let him use that time to benefit his children or his marriage.

The alternative to missions-minded churches that are demanding of their missionaries is this: pastors and churches at home need to be more concerned with their communication with the missionary than they are the missionary's communication with them. It's not the missionary's job to encourage you to pray for him. It's the local church and their pastor's job to communicate with and encourage the missionary. That means much more than sending a cheque each month. If money is all the missionary needs, he can get that from the lost. There are plenty of un-churched people willing to help out with humanitarian-type efforts.

Though you ought to financially support your missionary in a very generous manner, the missionary doesn't really need your money. (God owns the cattle on a thousand hills and if you won't be faithful in giving, He will care for His servant and you will miss out on the blessing of being involved.) Much more than your money, *your missionary needs you!* He and his poor wife are out there all alone because you failed to send them in a team, and now you expect a one-way communication relationship. Take the initiative. Call, write, video-conference, and get on a plane and visit. That's the Biblical model. In the New Testament, we don't find churches demanding news from Paul. Instead, we find Paul, the spiritual father, writing to these little works thanking them for their help and giving them instructions for their assemblies. In truth, we find the seasoned pastor (Paul) checking in on and pouring time and love into his missions works.

Here's the point. If we are supposed to act like Jesus toward those whom He has put in our care, doesn't that also apply to the missionary? Shouldn't I care for/about my missionary as much as or more than those with whom I go to church?

Here is a question. If your missionary called you on the phone and didn't introduce himself, would you know him? Do you have so little contact with the man you have sent halfway around the world to represent your church that you wouldn't even recognize his voice? Can your missionary call and even get you on the phone? Can he open a conversation with, "Hi, it's me," and be assured that you know exactly who is on the other end of the line?

Another thought regarding our current "box" is this: Are we treating our missionaries like individuals, with individual needs or like widgets pumped out of a factory? So often church missions "policies" impose sterile, one-size-fits-all expectations upon missionaries with little or no concern for them as individuals. (Do you know how impossible it is for an individual missionary to keep up with all the supporting church's paperwork and policies? If an individual missionary has fifty supporting churches, that's fifty different sets of expectations he has to attempt to satisfy.)

As church leaders, we work alongside those on our team in the local church with deference to their individual personalities, strengths, weaknesses, and circumstances. Shouldn't we have the same individual care and extend the same latitude toward our missionaries? The problem is that if we have not taken the time to get to know our missionaries on a personal level, then we cannot format our care to their individual needs.

Blanket policies may be simple and efficient, but they do not reflect life. Life is messy and complicated with intricacy and nuance. We must accept messy and complicated. We must take up the challenge of caring individually for our missionary and getting into the trenches with them.

In my humble opinion, the local church should have no more missionaries than their congregation can effectively and personally care for, communicate with, and encourage.

Let's take a step backward for a moment from the mission field to deputation. (Deputation is that time frame in which missionaries go from church to church explaining what they believe God would have them do and raising support to do so.) In regard to this stage of missions there are currently two "boxes". The first is that strategy of going from church to church asking for financial support. The second is going to a mission agency and asking to be hired. Although there is technically nothing evil about these strategies, neither is a totally Biblical model.

The problem with deputation is that we "waste" two to four years of a missionary's life, and nearly a quarter of a million dollars before he/she ever goes to language school or moves to the mission field. (The word "waste" must be put in quotation marks here because I in no way wish to denigrate the ministry toward the local church that a missionary does in deputation. However, the goal here is raising money and raising awareness for prayer, not ministry to the individual local church primarily.)

In addition to the "waste" of the resources of time and money, our missionaries must brave dangerous highways and inclement weather conditions. Because of this (humanly speaking), we have buried some of our best missionaries (and sadly some of their precious children) along the deputation trail long before they ever made it to the mission field.

This is a problem ("waste" and danger) that could be solved by means of technology, trust, and a higher level of cooperation among the churches. That however, would mean that churches and church leaders would have to put pride, pettiness, and personal preference aside for the cause of Jesus Christ in this world.

The problem with going to a missions agency and asking to be hired to do missions work (usually this is a humanitarian-type mission) is that it bypasses the local church (God's program for today) altogether. Although it fixes the problem of wasted time and finance, it does not answer the need of a wide base of prayer partners and the Biblical care of local churches for the individual missionary.

The logical conclusion is that the "deputation experience" could be done in a simpler, more Biblical, common sense way.

In our current box, we want all the missionaries to plant churches that look and sound like our own; no matter the cultural, or situational differences between home and mission field. The missions teams of the New Testament understood that if a church was going to grow in native soil that it was not going to be (apart from the gospel) exactly the same as the sending church.

The concept of reproducing ourselves somewhere else is not a credible theory. It is Jesus who reproduces Himself. If you reproduce yourself, you reproduce your flaws as well. If you get out of the way and allow Jesus to reproduce Himself in the church plant or missions church, there is nothing but good that comes from that!

In the natural world, if you change the soil that the plant is in, you ultimately change the makeup of the plant. Different soil has different properties, different elements, nutrients, pollutants, and moisture levels. Therefore, different soil gives you a similar but different plant. What we really should be spreading is the gospel (not our traditions, ideas, cracks, and faults), and then we can leave how the new church looks and sounds up to God and the new native congregation. To expect exact conformity means that we haven't taken the realities of the situation into consideration and haven't thought this through.

The idea that a missions church in Africa, or for that

matter over in the next town, must be a cookie cutter copy of yours is impractical and unBiblical. This is a relatively new concept; stemming first from England's colonization of much of the world in the 1800's and more recently from modern businesses franchising their stores. Every McDonald's you go into is essentially identical whether you are in Hong Kong or New York City. Therefore, you are comfortable because it is familiar.

Churches are different. They are not supposed to all be alike. You aren't supposed to be comfortable in a church plant or missions work in another culture. City folks aren't comfortable in the country and the country people would rather chew their arm off than live in the concrete jungle. That's not to say that either the city or the country is bad, they are just different!

The missionary's job is not to conform a church in Scandinavia to the comfort level of someone from North Carolina. A missions church must be geared for the glory of God and the evangelization of the people and culture in which it finds itself. That means that the visiting pastor from the home church might be a little uncomfortable with a few things. Really now, a different place, race, language, people, and culture; what else did you expect?

As is evident from our discussion, the "box" that we find ourselves in today in regard to missions is not wholeheartedly in line with the first-century church. It is a box of our own making. Therefore, we have the right and responsibility to set fire to it. If we don't, God eventually will do it for us, but that will be much more painful for all involved. Let's get back to "before the box."

7. OUR APPROACH TO CULTURE BEFORE THE BOX

Very often, the tendency of Christianity is to try to "freeze" Christianity within those times that were most favorable to it by trying to recreate that past era in the present culture. We do this by trying to duplicate the ministry methods that we believe were responsible for the spiritual uptick seen in that bygone era.

In our time frame, the era that we in Christianity seem to want to recreate is the 1950's. That era has become idealized and idolized in the mind of popular culture and the heart of many Christians.

But there were practical reasons that the 1950's were culturally conservative as well as conducive to spiritual progress. World War Two had just ended, and we in North America believed that we won because God was on our side – which He was. However, we did not win the war against fascism and imperialism because God approved of all that we were doing. (i.e., the culture of society and the church culture and activity in the 40's and 50's)

Despite innocent portrayals of these decades, the reality was that sin was still a disease that festered just under the surface of the genteel society of the time. During those days, sin hid behind closed doors and behind a façade of church-going morality. Although there have been seasons (like the 1940's and 50's) where the culture as a whole has been more moralistic than others, this does not mean that the sinful heart of man took a vacation. Sin has been present in every era. To look back fondly on the "good old days" imagining that they were free from evil and wickedness is a mistake.

I remember watching the television show "Happy Days". It was set in the late 1950's and early 60's. Even as a child I was smart enough to know that they weren't all happy days. Although the times were more innocent than today, there was still more than enough sin and evil to go around.

Following World War Two, we discover that another effect of the war was taking shape within the church. When the boys came home from the war, many followed God's call into the ministry (for their sacrifice both to the country and to the ministry of Christ we will forever be grateful). These men had a clarity of purpose that had been forged in the fire of war. Their passion for the Gospel of Jesus Christ and love for souls was undeniable.

One of the unintended consequences of having this wave of former soldiers as preachers was what we will call the "regimentalization" of the church. Because these preachers believed with all their hearts that God had given them the victory in the war, they assumed that it was His stamp of approval on the culture of the war years and more specifically the militaristic life of rules that had governed their every waking moment and every action.

This then led to a regimented culture within the church. If

rules could not be found in the Bible to cover some specific aspect of life, they made up a rule and found a verse (many times, unfortunately, pulled out of context) to support their position. These men prized order and discipline and embedded their brand of regimented Christianity into the churches for generations to come.

The sixties, of course, was the decade that challenged the church as a whole and more specifically, challenged this newly ordained batch of thousands of G.I. preachers. These were the men who sounded the alarm against the moral landslide that defined that decade. Their certainty amid an uncertain time allowed the church as a whole to come into the seventies ready to walk contrary to a now amoral culture. There was, of course, the baggage of some overreaching rules and a cookie-cutter approach to the church and the Christian walk of the individual that we now struggle to address. However, we should be grateful and see the hand of God as He used these men in their place in time.

It was in this era that the stage was set for the vast expansion of the evangelical church from the seventies into the nineties as the church caught onto the idea (if not the name) of duplicating churches like businesses sell and build franchises. All of the infrastructure was there. The rules and procedures had been pounded out in triplicate. Each new church was a carbon copy of the last.

The effect of this was that we created a Christian subculture that looked much like the 1950's within current society (the 70's through to the 90's) believing that in doing so we had the best chance of re-achieving the cultural ideal of the 50's that really wasn't.

The faulty assumption that we made is that it was the culture and ministry methods of the time that brought society closer to God rather than the hand of God doing the work. In this, we are sadly mistaken. If we look at history, we can see God using the Great Depression of the 30's and World War Two to move us away from the ungodliness and amoral decadence of the "roaring twenties." He made North America both dependent upon Himself in the Great Depression, and then in World War Two, we became an influence worldwide. This would prove extremely useful in the missions efforts in the coming decades.

Sometime in the 1970's, a movement began in the churches that understood that a Christian subculture based on the 1950's was not going to be effective long term in reaching modern society. Unfortunately, this group of churches, by and large, allowed the pendulum of popular thought within the churches to swing to the opposite extreme. They began to teach that the Christians had to immerse themselves in present day culture (the good, the bad, the questionable, and the ugly) in order to reach modern people. This, of course, led to rapid erosion of standards and separation in the name of being "relevant" to society.

The problem with this approach was that in order to be "just one of the guys," Christians had to involve themselves in the thought, language, and activities of those around them— whether it was godly or not.

This wave of thought is a direct descendant of the failed "in them to win them" strategy. Ill-advised men employed this method in the 1920's and onward attempting to infiltrate and change liberal and modernist denominations. The modern incarnation of this idea is that if the Christian just talked the same, walked the same, and participated in the same activities as the unchristian that they would be accepted and so would their message.

Biblically speaking, the problem with this logic is that "we" (Christians) are not like "them" (unchristians) on an elemental level. We can dress like them, eat their food, participate in their entertainment, and have appreciation for some aspects of their culture. But we have been made *"new creatures" (Second Corinthians 5:17) and "citizens" (Ephesians 2:19)* of a different Kingdom. So, any attempt to be "relevant" by absorbing and adapting to the whole of current culture would simply be hypocritical on the part of a genuine child of God.

With an understanding of the historical context we can then look with more clarity upon the issues that face the church when it comes to the culture of today.

The first thing that we realize is that Biblically God has not called us to create a "Christian subculture," but instead has called us to recognize that we are "new creatures" (a race of different people) that are citizens of a different kingdom. We have not been called to adapt to current culture nor have we been ordered to withdraw from it.

The Great Commission gives us a bigger, more Biblical approach to culture. Our approach to culture is that of an *"ambassador." (Second Corinthians 5:20)* The American ambassador to Zambia may live in Zambia, participate in parts of Zambian culture, and eat Zambian food. However, he knows that he is not a Zambian and that his mission is to represent the United States of America.

Because of his purpose in this foreign country, there may be aspects of Zambian culture, and daily life in which he cannot participate and still effectively represent the United States government.

As we take the Biblical example to its logical conclusion,

we come to the understanding that God has not called us to assimilate or to withdraw, but rather we are here to represent a heavenly kingdom and the culture of that kingdom to this present world.

This means that no matter how precious our memories of past "Christian friendly" eras, it is not our calling to recreate those times nor is it our mandate to spend time and energy pining for those times past.

On the other hand, because we are ambassadors of the kingdom we cannot "go native" and dive headlong into the culture of our time without discerning what level of participation in this foreign (not kingdom) culture will best help us represent our King Jesus and the kingdom of heaven.

8. THE GOSPEL BEFORE THE BOX

It has become apparent over the years that what we commonly call "the gospel" has been watered down to the point where anyone that has prayed a prayer and says, "I love Jesus" is considered by others to be a Christian. Strictly speaking, the apostle Paul defines the gospel as the good news; the death, burial, resurrection, and soon coming of Jesus Christ. *(First Corinthians 15)* That is the good news!

For the most part, it is not the good news itself that has been diluted, but rather the expected human response to the gospel has been diluted. Remember what Jesus said? His first statement in the book of Mark is, *"The time is fulfilled, and the kingdom of God is at hand: repent ye, and believe the gospel." (Mark 1:15)*

Unfortunately, because of the desire for an easy Christianity and the unrelenting drive for numbers and crowds at the church house, we have seen a dilution of the Biblical expected human response to the gospel. No longer is repentance mentioned from the pulpit in connection to the gospel. Belief is preached, but seldom do we hear that true belief in Christ necessarily includes repenting of your own way and turning to His ways.

Lest we get confused, let's put forward a Biblical definition of repentance.

Repentance is a change of heart, mind, and will in regard to sin, self, and God. *(Acts 26:20; Matthew 3:8)*

The act of repentance itself is internal. The fruits, or the outworking of repentance (right actions) are external. This culminates in changed life.

The idea of repentance is not the action of quitting all our sin. The idea of repentance is that a change of our heart and mind has set a trajectory in our lives that makes us desire to work each day to rid sin from our lives and introduce good actions. When Jesus included repentance as part of the expected response to the gospel, He was not calling for a works- based salvation, but rather was calling for a deep change in the core level thinking and direction of His audience. He was asking them to change their outlook regarding themselves, their sin, their religious traditions, and their concept of God. This core level change of thinking (or change of heart) is what Jesus summed up in the word "repent." The obvious outworking of that repentance is continual changes in behavior over a lifetime as we are daily transformed by the Word and the power of the Holy Spirit into the image of Jesus Christ.

In **Luke fourteen** we find Jesus telling the unsaved multitudes to **"count the cost."** It is this very "cost" that we fail to communicate in relation to the gospel today.

We have changed the gospel from something that is very

demanding (demanding a core level change of thinking and direction - repentance) to something that is emotionally and mentally easier than joining a country club. Jesus said that part of the decision for salvation was counting the cost. In that day, "counting the cost" meant that families may disown you, employers may fire you, governments may persecute you, and friends may abandon you. When was the last time that the cost of believing the gospel was proclaimed from our pulpits?

Unfortunately, obeying Jesus by "counting the cost" of becoming a believer is neglected in the vocabulary of the pulpits of North America in our day because in North America, Christianity has been in a place of power (the majority) for the past two hundred years or so. (That has now changed as what we know as "Christendom" is giving way to postmodern/pre- paganism in North America.) The preaching of "counting the cost" and repentance as part of the choice to follow Jesus has been replaced by a "believe easy and live easy" Christianity that places no demands on the Christian other than adherence to a moral code practiced and expected by the sub-culture of their church.

We often wonder why more people aren't following Jesus into His mission. Why are our churches full of people who are willing to sit and be entertained while a few do the actual work of ministry and evangelism? The answer is simple. We have many people in our churches that just are not saved. They know the lingo. They know the songs. They know how to behave well enough to fit into the church, but they don't really know Jesus. Their core thinking and direction has never changed. They have given mental assent to the Christ of history but have never obeyed the Christ of the Bible as He called them to repentance.

Remember these words? ***"Many will say to me in that***

day, Lord, Lord, have we not prophesied in thy name? and in thy name have cast out devils? and in thy name done many wonderful works? And then will I profess unto them, I never knew you: depart from me, ye that work iniquity." (Matthew 7:22-23)

How then do we begin to right the ship? How do we proclaim a salvation that is by grace through faith alone while including teaching on the inextricable truths of the necessity of repentance and the cost of discipleship? What we have to understand is that these concepts are not mutually exclusive, but rather are pieces of the same beautiful puzzle.

We are not saved by works (the fruits of repentance) but by our belief in Christ's finished work on the cross. However, one who has not truly repented has not truly believed.

Belief in Christ necessarily requires obedience to His command to repent. They (belief and repentance) are inseparably linked. Whether one realizes it at the moment of true salvation or not, if that individual has truly believed in Christ he has also repented of belief in himself (his **"own way" – Isaiah 53:6**), his sins, his religious traditions and his gods. This is the arithmetic of salvation. One side of the equation (belief) necessitates that the other side (repentance) be in balance.

Again, repentance is to be defined as "a change of heart, mind, and will in regard to sin, self, and God."

That does not mean that at the moment of salvation we become people who no longer sin, but we do become people who no longer want to stay in sin. Repentance is that core level change in direction.

Too many of our converts are just that, our converts. We have convinced people that being a Christian is the best way to live a productive, happy life. After all, everyone wants to think that God is on their side. Much of this "Christian life" is portrayed to be what we do, like going to church, reading our Bibles, helping others, praying, etc… instead of who we are and what God is doing in us. This emphasis on the outward has made it very easy for people who want a *"form of godliness" (Second Timothy 3:5)* and the promise of an easier life to sign onto the membership of our churches. In fact, much of our preaching is geared to this "believe easy and live easy" doctrinal error.

There was nothing easy about the choice to believe Jesus in the early church. To the culture at large, Jesus was not a hero, but rather a joke. In addition to this, governments and religious leaders were engaged in stamping out the belief in Christ by means of violence.

We cannot today make the decision to follow Christ any easier than it was back then. Yes, the message is simple -- *"Repent and Believe the Gospel" (Mark 1:15)*. Yes, all the work for our salvation was done on the cross. Jesus paid all of the price. Because of that, salvation is a free gift.

Repentance and counting the cost of belief are not works that get us to heaven. In truth, they are not works at all but part of the process of thinking and decision making as one settles upon their new direction by choosing to truly follow Jesus by faith. Repentance and counting the cost (culminating in simple faith) are essential elements of the correct response to the good news of Jesus Christ.

When the Bible tells us, *"And they said, Believe on the Lord Jesus Christ, and thou shalt be saved…" (Acts*

16:31). It is not neglecting repentance and counting the cost of belief. Instead, it is assuming that these two aspects of belief are present. In the first century, becoming a Christian was not a simple decision to make. Many would lose their lives because of that choice. Therefore, those early believers were acutely aware that they were "repenting" (mentally and emotionally turning and taking a totally different direction) and they certainly were totally informed, by what was occurring in their society, as to the cost that becoming a true believer and follower of Christ would demand. And yet, thousands did "count the cost" and did "repent and believe."

Today, the church must free itself from its obsession with numbers and dollars to once again preach repentance, belief, and a walk with Jesus that will cost you everything. This is the way we move people from spectators of the mission to those who are totally dedicated to the mission.

This is a box in which we cannot allow ourselves to continue to be trapped. The souls of thousands of people, even in our own churches, are at stake. Also in the balance hangs the glory of God. God is glorified not when people are willing to believe on Jesus based upon the subtly communicated promises of an easy Christian life now and Heaven someday, but rather He is glorified when people choose Him despite the recognition of the reality of the high cost of turning from themselves, their own way, and their sin to follow Jesus.

The box that we are currently occupying demands rent that is much too high for us to continue to pay. Counting the cost and repentance culminating in belief comprise the Biblical response of the individual to the gospel, the good news, and result in true salvation. This is the message that we must proclaim.

9. GOOD WORKS BEFORE THE BOX

Jesus *"went about doing good" (Acts 10:38)*. Why then do most Christians think that they are exempt from good works? Oh, they wouldn't say that out loud, but in reality that's how their life plays out.

Some avoid helping the sick, the poor, the disadvantaged, the orphan, and the widow because they don't see the link between good works and delivering the gospel (the GOOD news) to those that are hurting.

Others aren't involved in good works because they are just bone lazy. There are those who would like to be involved in good works, but their church leadership isn't providing clear guidance and opportunities in the area so those people without direction just give up.

Then there are still others who feel that money given to good works is "wasted" in light of eternity. They see no need to expend the resources of the church to be a physical help when the greater need is spiritual – the salvation of the soul. However, if Jesus had this same attitude, He would not have bothered to "do good". Surely Jesus had His priorities in order.

For all of these reasons and more, good works are being neglected in our churches today. And in those few churches that are geared toward being a practical help to others, there are those members who have decided to "outsource" their obligation to the pastors, deacons, missionaries, and benevolent boards within the church by means of monetary gifts.

After all, for most in our society it is far easier to drop a few dollars in the plate for the orphanage than it is for them to take time out of their schedule to help in the orphanage kitchen. It is easier, but not rewarding, and not right.
The giving of token amounts of money to salve our own conscience is a copout. God has called all of us to be personally invested in others.

God has called us to good works. Titus tells us that Jesus *"...gave himself for us, that he might redeem us from all iniquity, and purify unto himself a peculiar people, zealous of good works." (Titus 2:14)*

Jesus told us that good works were the way to bring attention to the gospel and glory to God. *"Let your light so shine before men, that they may see your good works, and*
glorify your Father which is in heaven." (Matthew 5:16)

Matthew 25:34-46 teaches us that we serve Jesus by serving others. We have to be concerned for and work for the benefit of the *"least of these"*. If we do not, we are not following the command and the heart of Christ. To simply argue that the only thing God cares about is the salvation of the human soul is to negate large chunks of the Word of God.

Just take time to read through all of the verses that talk of the orphan, the widow, the poor, and the fatherless. God will use those verses to break your heart for the needs around you.

God wants all men to be saved. But because God loves all men, He asks us to display His love by means of good works so that He may receive the glory that He is due.

There are two different boxes that many of our churches have ended up in today. Neither of which are Biblically balanced. The first box says, "Do good; don't worry about proclaiming the gospel with words. They'll get it eventually." The favourite quotation of those within this camp is "Preach the gospel, and if necessary, use words." This quotation is most often mistakenly attributed to Francis of Assisi,[10] and it is venerated by many on nearly the same level as Scripture.

The other box says, "Don't worry about feeding, housing, and healing the hurting. Just preach the gospel. Let the unsaved deal with all the do-gooder stuff" Of course, this is never said out loud, much less from the platform. But as we look at the church's missions projects, home charity work, and budget, we find that the disturbing truth is that this is the mindset of those within this box.

Both of these attitudes are boxes from which we must escape. God cares about the poor, the abused, the neglected, and the hurting. He expects us to help them. He expects them to see Himself in us, and He expects us to open our mouths and proclaim the gospel to the hurting.

John wondered whether Jesus really was the Messiah that was promised. Jesus told John's followers, ***"Go your way, and tell John what things ye have seen and heard; how that the blind see, the lame walk, the lepers are cleansed, the deaf hear, the dead are raised, to the poor the gospel*** *is preached." (Luke 7:22)*

The Bible teaches us that we must put a priority upon the proclamation of the gospel. However, we must give proper attention to good works. Good works play a role in the proclamation of the gospel, in the display of God's love, and in the glorification of God.

10. SEPARATION BEFORE THE BOX

In our day, the doctrine of separation has become loved by some tribes within Christianity and despised by others. Both extremes have shut themselves into a "box" that was not envisioned by the writers of Scripture. Let's take them one at a time.

The first box is the isolationist box. Those who choose to shut themselves up in this box see the verses of Scripture that highlight separation through the lenses of their own experience, traditions, peer-pressure, and teachings.

Many times, the isolationist will engage in "proof texting" in order to make their case to separate from cooperation with those who differ with them on relatively minor things.

What we mean by "proof texting" is the process of deciding first what side you are on regarding any given topic and then going to look for Bible verses to support your pre-conceived position. Most times in this practice, the context of the verses in question are ignored so that the "proof text" can be used as a simplistic answer to a more complex Biblical question. It is a form of lazy scholarship. This is dangerous in many ways, but ultimately its danger comes from setting up one man (or a group of men that think the same way), or one popular publication as the authority, and the chief applicator of Scripture for their association, denomination, or tribe.

The Bible says that it is of **"no private interpretation." (Second Peter 1:20)** That means that no one can claim that a verse means something that isn't readily apparent from the context and the plain reading of the verse itself. In addition, this verse implies that the "public" interpretation of a verse is to be accepted.

In the debate over separation (whether it be what erring ministry to separate from, what activity to separate from, or what people to separate from), it is essential that each verse that refers to separation is seen in its proper context. Simply doing this, will at least get the isolationist to think about the broader scope of the Bible in relation to separation instead of cherry picking the verses that suit his viewpoint.

Is the goal to get the isolationist to suddenly be cooperating with those Christians and churches whose beliefs and practices are far outside of his comfort zone? No, my goal is to get the isolationist to once again engage in culture and interact with the people around him so that he may effectively model Jesus and proclaim the Gospel. It is very hard to model Christ and communicate the gospel from the self-made box of the isolationist because by definition he has excluded from his daily life those whom he claims to be trying to reach.

You see, the isolationist separatist sees Christianity as kind of a castle with a moat. Once a week, he lowers the drawbridge and rides out into battle armed with the gospel in hopes of bringing back a few "captives" for Christ into the castle. His separatist views of Scripture have given him such a hatred for sin that he cannot stand sinners. This, of course drags the isolationist separatist into a catch twenty-two. He can't be around sinners because they sin. But he's not around sinners so he can't talk to them about Jesus, and no one gets saved.

So, the isolationist separatist relies on brief forays onto the battlefield of evangelism   instead of making the mission of Christ a part of his daily life within the current culture and around people that disagree with him. With this method (brief evangelistic crusades and weekly attempts at spreading the gospel in the community) he can feel good about his obedience to the great commission *(Matt. 28:18-20)* while avoiding the meaningful, daily contact of being involved in the daily lives of those outside of his Christian sub-culture.

The other feel-good avenue that the isolationist takes in regard to reaching the lost is money. Money for advertisement of special meetings and church events becomes the balm that soothes the isolationist separatist's discomfort with his self-inflicted catch twenty- two. When no one comes to his meetings and church events, he assures himself of the rightness of his ways by saying, "No one wants to follow Jesus anymore." But maybe, just maybe, they would follow Jesus if they saw someone following Jesus through the mud of daily life with them instead of just the Christian advertisements that money can buy.

Now that we have described the one extreme, let's move on to the box that lies at the other extreme. This is the box of permissiveness and lack of restraint.

The individual in this box also sees the Scriptures through their own myopic lens. Usually someone promoting this position takes a more general view of the Scriptures and doesn't delve too much into detail. The idea of studying the Scriptures and applying them to each situation of life is almost discouraged in this box. The fear, of course, is that if they were to search out the Bible for an answer regarding what activities, practices, and people to separate from, they might have to actually separate. Those in this box seem to bypass or excuse verses like Second Corinthians 6: 14, First Corinthians 6:19-20, and the many list that Paul gives of sinful and immoral activity in a desperate bid to do what "feels right" to them. For these people, love is synonymous with unity, and "tough love" is never in their vocabulary. John chapter seventeen is their guiding passage to the exclusion of other Scriptures that shed light on and give definition to Jesus' prayer, and "unity" becomes the highest goal.

Those who follow a permissive approach to separation most times refuse to recognize the challenges of their position. One challenge is that if permissiveness is the God ordained plan for the Christian life, how does one know where to draw the line? In fact, are there any lines at all? In the end, the humanistic thinking of "You do what's right for you; I'll do what's right for me as long as no one gets hurt," becomes the mantra of the permissive. Because there is no one willing to draw a line of separation, then cooperation with anyone and any doctrine becomes not only permissible but encouraged.

Another challenge that faces the permissive is that morality becomes subjective. If one refuses to look to the Bible for principles to guide communication, partnership, cooperation, behavior, and entertainment, then there is no authority, and everyone can make up their own rules.

The problem with the box of the permissive is that, in the end, they end up with no borders to their "country" and then throw up their hands in bewilderment when the enemy comes marching up their street, knocks on their door, and asks to come in for tea. More startling yet, is the truth that some, because of their ultra- permissive outlook, have entertained the enemy and have been taken captive by Satan's wiles and are utterly oblivious to their dire situation.

In the end, some happy medium must be found on the

level ground of Biblical common sense that lies between these two boxes. God has given us a Book. That Book contains direct instruction and principles that we can apply to guide our lives.

We need not look to find a verse for every situation. To do so would necessitate what Peter called twisting the Scriptures. *(I Pet 3:16)* Nor should we simply assume that there is no verse that applies and do whatever we desire. In the middle ground of Biblical common sense, we find that the Bible does have principles that we can apply with discernment to issues of personal separation and direct statements that guide our ecclesiastical (church ministry) separation.

Over the years, the issues that fall under the title of separation have become the hot issue. Especially between those who have staunchly taken up a position in either the isolationist or permissive boxes.

We have talked to some degree about the history of the conservative evangelical Christian churches. Let's look at some sociological reasons why they have fortified their box and drawn battle lines.

Around the 1920's, good men had to take a hard stand against a liberalism within the churches, denominations, and especially the colleges and seminaries that had denied or questioned some of the doctrines central to the faith; such things as the inerrancy of the Bible and the virgin birth of Christ. These great men understood that the very foundation of Christianity was at stake, and they took the hard stand that was necessary. From this era the phrase "militant fundamentalism" developed. Although the term sounds harsh to the modern ear, at the time, it denoted men who would take a stand. These heroes were used by God to save North America from the steep slide into liberalism that we saw in Europe.

By the time World War Two was over the battle had pretty much been waged over the core doctrines or the "fundamentals" of the faith. The 1950's were, for the most part, a time of men getting back from the war, getting educations, starting families, and healing from both the physical and emotional wounds of war. By the time the 1960's rolled around with all of its political and cultural upheaval the preachers of the North American churches were ready for another fight. With the battle over the core doctrines won, it was now time to put Christian values center stage. Drugs, sex, and rock and roll climbed to a fever pitch (or so it seemed at the time) and the threat of communism was an ever present reality, so there was a lot to preach about.

With this new, surging, and valid threat to the youth of the nation, preachers came out fighting (and rightly so) against the downward moral spiral of the day.

As we have previously noted, many men that had come home from the war got their Bible college degrees with the help of the G.I. Bill. About 2.2 million veterans used the G.I. Bill to go to college and university. Obviously, the veterans who had gotten their Bible college or seminary training were also deeply ingrained with the militaristic training of outward discipline from their time in the armed services. This militaristic outlook and discipline was the new method to go along with the new battleground for the church.

It wasn't long before there was a regulation (and a Bible verse -- not necessarily interpreted or applied well) for everything you could think of. Everything, that is, except that which was truly at stake...the heart. This began a forty year trend in conservative Christianity of regulating the outward man without giving serious attention to renewing the inward man.

To be fair, there were those within conservative

Christianity that had balance in this area, but as a whole, the pendulum swung heavily toward conformation instead of transformation.

This brings us to another observation concerning the isolationist vs. the permissive. As we have noted, the conservative/isolationist's historically have done very well at teaching the regulation of behavior. At the other end of the spectrum, in the box of the permissive camp, we find a historical reliance on feelings as a guiding light. So, one box taught people how to act, and the other taught them how to feel, but neither (as a whole) did well with teaching people how to think.

So, back to our historical narrative.

In the 1980's, we began to see the results of this as conservative leaders began to fall as a result of leading double lives. Simply regulating outward action with Biblical truth was not sufficient It was a tragic time for North American Christianity, and in the public mind, Christianity has yet to fully recover the trust betrayed.

Meanwhile in the permissive box...

In the early 1990's a few churches began to make a national name for themselves by throwing out separation entirely (both personal and ecclesiastical) while, at least in theory, maintaining the core doctrines that were defended so capably in the 1920's. These mega-churches attempted to make the church "user friendly" and approachable for the unsaved. Under this mandate nearly everything was permissible in the church as long as it appealed to unchurched people and drew a crowd. Although these churches gained many followers and much fame, the challenges of their position were numerous (most notably the fact that their guiding theory was focused on what the unsaved man wanted in a church and not necessarily what God wanted), and over time their theories have proven not to be healthy and difficult to defend.

And so we arrive at today. Today, there are still those who resort to one box or the other – to either separatist isolation or to liberal permissiveness.

As we consider what things were like before the box, let's make a few general statements.

Ecclesiastical Separation:

Before the box (really before 1970), you weren't considered a heretic or a compromiser if you fellowshipped with a church that wasn't in your camp or denomination as long as they were "orthodox" (believed in the fundamentals of the faith) in their doctrine. In fact, most of the men that preachers today quote from the pulpit, and read/learn from privately are not from their own tribe or denomination.

Before the box, there were those preachers and churches from different denominational camps who could cooperate with each other to one extent or another based on the core doctrines of the Word of God. These men were gentlemen enough not to emphasize their differences in secondary issues while guests in each other's pulpits. These were the great statesmen whose writings, sayings, and sermons were quoted for the next half century. While willing to do battle for those things that were central (life and death) to the faith, they were not willing to divide the ranks of Christianity concerning issues over which good, godly men honestly disagreed.

Personal Separation:

In order to get to "before the box" in the area of personal separation, we have to literally go back to the first century. We must do this because there have been very few times in history when true Christian individual soul liberty and the priesthood of the believer were allowed to be exercised.

Let's look at the **Book of Acts**. In **chapter fifteen**, a bunch of Jewish Christians were all worked up because Gentile Christians weren't following all the rules they thought that they should. Now, understand, the Jews had some pretty good rules that enforced what we would consider "Christian morality" very well. (By the way, all the religions and the cults have good moral rules that create people who act "Christian-like.") So, in order to determine what regulations to levy upon the new Gentile believers the church leaders got together and had a big meeting. In the end they only gave those believers who had not grown up in the very restrictive Jewish faith just four rules.

They were:
1. Don't worship idols.
2. Don't fornicate.
3. Don't eat anything that was strangled.
4. Don't drink blood.

The apostles could have laid it heavy on the Gentile Christians, but they did not. They could have regulated their lives by telling them what forms of entertainment they could enjoy and what activities they could partake in, but they did not. They could have told them that they had to follow the Jewish laws so everybody could "be on the same page," "get along," and so that no one would "be offended." But they did not.

Even in Paul's letters he (a Pharisee who knew and personally followed hundreds of Jewish rules) did not try to regulate and enforce outward compliance but instead spent the majority of his time talking about what Peter calls the *"hidden man of the heart." (First Peter 3:4)* Paul knew that the heart was the issue. If the heart was right, the outside would follow eventually. An apple does not ripen from the outside to the inside; neither do Christians.

Having said all of that, in the local church there is the necessary and voluntary submission to spiritual leaders. *(Hebrews 13:17)* Because of this, a wise leader will know what issues are church issues, what issues Biblically lie in under the authority of the husband (the leader of the home), and what issues to leave between the individual and the Holy Spirit.

In the church, there must be enough common ground in the area of personal separation for individuals in leadership or on staff to be able to work comfortably with each other, and enough commonalities in belief between staff and congregation to walk together. So a wise leader, like the church council at Jerusalem, will define some basic, common ground in the area of separation for the purpose of working together for Christ. This must, however, be exercised with humble wisdom and not be seen as being "lords over God's heritage."

Neither as being lords over God's heritage, but being ensamples to the flock. (1 Peter 5:3)

In other words, God has not authorized spiritual leadership in churches to be micromanagers of other's lives. That's the Holy Spirit's job.

The problem of micromanagement in many churches has arisen as a result of schools and Bible colleges directly affiliated with a local church. The challenge is that the strictly regimented personal separation and studious dedication that is necessarily put in place to effectively educate and train young people is not conducive to the exercise of individual liberty and the priesthood of the believer in the congregation. But in order to be consistent, the church insists on the same level of commitment from church membership as from those in training. If they are not willing to uphold the same level of separation, they cannot serve in or through their church. This puts everyone into the same crucible of ministry boot camp.

Unfortunately, many times in those situations it is only the staff and the students that can or are willing to "live up" to these rigorous demands in order to be "qualified" to be involved in the ministries of the church. As a result, much of the congregation in such a situation sits in the pew like a mighty sleeping army never feeling worthy to fight.

It is in this vacuum of limited personal liberty that the seeds of discontent are sown because serving in the church has been embedded by God in the DNA of every believer. Being restricted from doing so because of a regimented philosophy geared toward the model of an educational institution instead of an organic congregation does harm to the average church member.

Even those educational institutions that are not directly affiliated with one individual local church have contributed to the difficulty. Simply put, they forget to tell their graduates, "Now you are going out into the real world where real people live their real lives with real problems and real nuances. So, take it easy on them."

Instead, well-meaning Bible colleges and seminaries send out bright, articulate, idealistic young pastors who believe that they learned the "formula" of "how to do it right" in college or seminary. The graduate then arrives at his new church with that same regimented, institutional philosophy that was modeled in during his educational days. This, of course, is entirely done out of a pure heart. Their college or seminary said (at least by example) that this formula would give them "success." This "formula" includes, among a dozen other things, the "only right way" of separation.

Generally, in the application of this college- given strategy no real thought is given to the individual needs and many varied situations of their congregants. Again, this leaves people out that could be involved in ministry in some fashion, sows the seeds of discontent and distrust, and makes those to whom you minister feel like simply a cog in the wheel of the minister's "successmobile." (Yes, I made that word up. Contact *Webster's!*)

11. YOUTH BEFORE THE BOX

Looking back on my childhood, I now realize that I was the luckiest kid of my generation. Simply put, I had parents that took their job to raise their children in the *"nurture and admonition of the Lord" (Eph 6:4)* seriously. They in turn, had a church that backed them up in that endeavor.

The systematic theology that I learned in Bible college and my personal study in the years since pales in comparison to what I learned as a child in nightly family devotions. Family was where my walk with Jesus began, and it was my parents who took the time to lay that foundation. Christianity was not an add-on for my parents; it was woven throughout their lives consistently; both public and private. My parents made wise decisions in controlling my world as a child and teen so that I could grow up protected, loved, and stable.

Unfortunately, as I look across the panorama of Christianity today, this example is the exception and not the norm. Today what we see is parents handing off the spiritual training of their children to the Sunday school, the Christian school, youth group, and the church.

We have tried everything with youth in a desperate attempt to keep them from leaving the church. We have tried to educate them, filling them with all kinds of Bible knowledge and trivia. This has made them into educated sinners. We have tried to entertain them with activities, music, and fun that appeals to them. This has made them into entitled, consumeristic sinners. We have tried to empathize with them saying things like, "It's so hard to be a young person these days," (just note that this is not the hardest time in history for a young person to grow up and stand for Jesus). In our empathy, we have made them emotional wrecks of self-pity and self- centeredness.

What we haven't done is look at the example of Jesus in the Word of God. My question to you is, "How did Jesus' fathers treat him as a young man?"

Look at Joseph. He involved Jesus in enterprise – he taught Jesus a trade. Idle hands really are the devil's workshop, and too many young people are allowed to grow up without basic life skills and without learning what it means to work and take responsibility.

Let's move from Jesus' earthly adopted father to His Heavenly Father. God the Father engaged Jesus in a mission. As a matter of fact, Jesus used the word *"sent" (John 20:21)* when He spoke of the direction of the Father upon His life.

A young person without a mission makes themselves (their wants and desires) the mission. The reason we live with so many narcissistic, consumeristic, anarchistic young people is that the generation that preceded them (parents) have not involved them in the mission of God.

I am thrilled when I see parents taking their young people down to the soup kitchen to feed the homeless or door to door to gather clothes to send to an overseas orphanage. My heart leaps for joy to see a young person mentored by their parent as that parent shares the gospel with a friend at a coffee shop.

In short, young people don't need more education, entertainment, or empathy. They need to be engaged in enterprise and mission. This is what it means to learn to be an adult, and that is what the teen years are supposed about; growing into adulthood.

So how did we get to this place where the parents have abdicated their God-given responsibility to the Sunday school, youth group, Christian school, and church?

It all dates back more than two hundred years to the beginning of the Sunday school movement. In the 1780's, Sunday school was developed to teach children reading, writing, mathematics, and the Bible. At this time, there was no publically available school nor were most of the parents educated enough to teach these things. The introduction of Sunday school, of course, solved a problem and put these children on track to better jobs and better lives, along with a solid concept of Christianity.

Fast forward now to the 1970's. Two significant developments are taking place in regard to youth within the churches. The first is the widespread acceptance of the Christian school. It seemed that from this time up through the late 1990's every church had to have either its own school or access to another church's school.

Alongside of this development, and not entirely separate from it, was the invention of a new office within the church. That being the "youth pastor." This usually consisted of some young fellow recently graduated from Bible college who had the energy to keep up with the young people's boundless energy in weekly "youth group" activities. The development of the "youth pastor" then slowly and subtly began to separate the church into demographics instead of families. The multigenerational church that had worked so well for so long (because it was Biblical) was subtly replaced by a demographically segmented church with each demographic vying for attention, dollars, and control.

So, with these new church "institutions" in place to teach the children how to be good little Christians, the parents were then freed to pursue the "American Dream." And pursue they did. After all, the professionals at the church, youth group, Christian school, and Sunday school could do a much better job at instilling spiritual truth and a daily walk with God into my children than I could, right?

It was also in the 1970's that across North American society church attendance by the fathers of families began to drop dramatically. The general idea was that church was for women and children. This alarming trend further gave the impression that the spiritual training of the children could be left up to the professionals at church.

On the whole, the 1980's and early 1990's were a boom for most of the North American economy. Chasing the American dream was never more popular, and the spiritual training of children by parents was neglected. After all, if the young people have all of the toys and gadgets they ever wanted and a lifestyle that is the envy of the rest of the world, what do they need of spirituality?

Giving your children "the best" became the name of the game and created a generation of parents that made little idols out of their children. They thought they were sacrificing to "give my children a better life." In reality, in many families, the children became the god of the parents. For many middle class families of this era, the majority of time, money, and effort was spent making sure little Johnny had everything he ever wanted. This only added to the self-centeredness of my generation.

This, of course, was the time when the youth group really began to take off. Consumerism was at its peak and the youth of North America were not immune to its allure. And so, because the church had chosen to define itself in terms of demographics rather than families it had to do all it could to keep "the youth" demographic.

So, churches pulled out all the stops and unfortunately made the same mistake as parents had in making an idol of the youth department. Many churches were (and still are) willing to sacrifice everything to appease the youth even if that sacrifice didn't please God.

It was in this era that nearly all boundaries of Biblical common sense were erased in the desperate pursuit of "keeping the youth in church." Looking back on it now, we realize that a focus on the youth was the easy thing to do, because we had the infrastructure set up to do it. (youth pastor, youth group, Christian school, Sunday school) Because of our demographic blinders, we neglected ministry to the family as a unit. Often this neglect led to, and still does lead to, disastrous consequence.

Today, in regard to youth, we exist in the hangover of history. We know that what we have done in the recent past in regard to youth hasn't worked well, but we are unsure as to what to do now. It's almost as if we have tried everything. I suggest that we look "before the box" for our answers.

As a part of the conversation concerning solutions, may I present some thoughts?

First, we are now in the third generation of parents that weren't parented well themselves. The skill of parenting has been turned over, in large part, to the entertainers and the professionals (aka: the church, the educators, and the medical community). Many parents have abdicated all responsibility but feeding, housing, and emotional support. Parents have to reclaim their role, and the church needs to be supportive of this.

Second, the focus of ministry has to be put back where Jesus had it; on the adults. You notice that he called adult men to follow Him first? Yes, I know that He said' *"Suffer the little children to come unto me," (Matthew 19:14)* but notice that it was the parents that were bringing those young ones. It wasn't a church program geared solely to that demographic apart from the family.

No matter how good the church, youth group, and school are they cannot replace the parents and family. No church will make progress on a large scale with the youth without making the parents and the family unit the ministry priority. God gave children parents long before He instituted anything else. A church with a holistic approach to the family focusing on the adults will, in time, do well with the youth.

Third, the church must work in tandem with the parents to give youth the opportunity and the impetus to be involved in both enterprise (work) and mission (service and evangelism). In this way, we point youth toward both responsible adulthood and the call of Jesus on their lives.

12. JESUS BEFORE THE BOX

The Jesus that is preached and taught in many churches today is a far cry from the Jesus of the Bible. The images people have of Jesus in their minds range from the rebel Jesus (as taught by some groups) to the effeminate concept of Jesus as depicted by others.

To get a clear picture of Jesus, we have to go "before the box." You see, all forms of art and media are useful, but in many ways, they have done a disservice to the image of Jesus that we have in our mind's eye. And, since it is His image that we are to emulate, we really do need to strive for accuracy. So, whether you are part of the "rebel rocker Jesus" group or the "effeminate, Jesus is only love" group, it is high time we ditch the boxes and see what Jesus really was like.

The pages of the Bible show us a man that is radically different from the paintings and epic film depictions of Christ. They show us a picture of a tradesman, a construction worker. Jesus was a man who knew what it was to have callouses on His hands and sweat on His forehead. Isaiah tells us that Jesus was not a man of outward beauty. *(Isaiah 53:2)* His were not the good looks of the "beautiful" leading men that have portrayed Him on film over the years.

Who a man chooses for his friends says a lot about who he is. Jesus chose the rough men of the sea. Not men who fished for sport, but men whose hands showed the wear from pulling on the ropes of the nets and whose skin was baked into a deep brown by the sunlight reflecting in searing rays off of the water of the Sea of Galilee. These were not men of refinement, but good hearty Israeli men who knew what it meant to put in a full day to feed their families. He chose a publican, a man who was despised by his culture. This showed his compassion. He chose two educated men, Luke the doctor and Paul the Jewish religious expert. This brings us to the man who introduced Jesus to the world. Jesus' cousin, John the Baptist was the rough prophet who came from a family that was part of the religious elite, the temple priests. This varied group of men shows us Jesus' ability to relate to those from diverse social strata.

It is true; we do see a caring, compassionate side of Jesus as well. We see Him weep at the tomb of Lazarus and as He looks out over Jerusalem. We see Him on the cross speaking to John to make sure that His mother would be cared for after His death. We see Him reach out with hands of healing toward the sick and diseased. We watch Him deal with people with love and patience.

Remember when Jesus said, "Follow me, and we will meet together each week and explore our feelings together so we can improve our lives"? Yeah, that didn't happen. Here's the point. Jesus was a man--not the Oprah of Galilee. In an effort to appeal to women (today, they seem to be the ones who choose what church the family goes to), churches have deemphasized the manly character and mindset of Christ to the point of its near extinction.

This is the balance that we see in Jesus. The man of a

rough blue-collar upbringing balanced with the dignity of a King who cares deeply for His subjects' welfare.

But in our talk about the heart of Jesus, we cannot forget that twice that heart led Him to carry a whip clearing the men from the temple that were ripping people off through currency exchange and overpriced merchandise. Balanced with that action, we see Jesus as the consummate teacher as He read and explained the Scriptures in that same temple.

The problem for us is that we want to simplify the image of Jesus into something that is easy for us to emulate. Therefore, if we just see Jesus as the one who turned established religion on its head, we can gripe about "the church," see ourselves as revolutionaries of Christianity, and think that we are like Jesus.

On the flip side, if we see Jesus only as a "all is love and sugar cookies" pacifist, then we are satisfied that we are like Him if we act like a doormat and let others walk all over us.

The thing we are missing in this conversation is the concept of "meekness." Jesus was meek. This is a word that is lost in our culture. If any have an idea of its definition, they usually associate it with weakness. Meekness, however, is far different. Meekness is power under control. Jesus was, and is, the God of the universe. He had, while on earth, the power that birthed all creation at His fingertips. And yet, He did not use it to take vengeance, but instead He went about *"doing good." (Acts 10:38)*

There was no halo that floated over Jesus' head as He walked down the street. He was, in human terms, an average Israeli man. He wouldn't have been tall and white with blue eyes as the movies suggest. But rather He would have been of average stature and build with the olive toned skin of the Middle East.

This same man, Jesus of Nazareth, shows up again in the **Book of the Revelation (19:11-16)**   riding on a horse as the Supreme Commander of the Armies of Heaven. He, through His perfect balance of manly strength, universal power, compassion, and love has earned the admiration and respect of the millions that have signed on to accept His good news and to follow His leadership.

The Jesus that we see "before the box" of Renaissance paintings and modern media is so much more interesting than the monochromatic image that pictures and movies produce. He is a man to follow, a friend to love, and a Saviour to believe. He is the multifaceted God of all Creation. To force Him into an image that simplifies Him just to satisfy our small minds, or worse, our own agendas is to make a Jesus of our own design...an idol.

13. THE CHURCH BEFORE THE BOX

Before the Western world's cultural box which we have lived in for the past several hundred years (Christendom), we find a very different church.

Before evangelical Christianity became the dominant religious force in England and then North America, churches operated differently. They did so because it was culturally a different time. My argument in this chapter is not for a specific church model, but rather, my argument is summed up in the following statement.

The first-century church (the one before the box) was incarnational, missional, organic, and nimble.

Before we move on, let me address the overuse and abuse of these terms. It seems these days that the words "incarnational," "missional," and "organic" have been adopted by conservatives and liberals alike. These individuals and churches have read into those terms whatever they wanted them to mean. This has led to some unChristlike and unscriptural things being done under their banner. Because of this, we unfortunately have to take time to frame our conversation by means of some definitions.

Now, let's look at each of these four descriptive words.

Incarnational – Jesus was God come to earth in the flesh (He became like us and into our culture) on a mission from His Father. This is the doctrine of the incarnation.

Some may balk at the use of the term "incarnational" in the sense that we will now use it, but if Jesus is our example in all things, it applies to some extent (and I believe a great extent) to how we should live in society. Because Christ is our example, we then strive to copy Christ in those aspects of His incarnation that we are able to copy. Think about it with me. We do have the Holy Spirit (God Almighty) living within us. God has made His temple in the hearts of His saints. In this sense, we too have God in flesh. We are not God, but God is in us in the person of the Holy Spirit. This is a beautiful picture that God has created in us of Jesus.

We do look like everyone else. We live in the culture of our day, and we should be living out the mission that God has sent us into the world to undertake. That's what Jesus did, and He did it without sinning. That is the human outworking of the doctrine of the incarnation as we emulate our Saviour. We carry God the Holy Spirit with us into our world carrying out the last command of Jesus to *"preach the gospel." (Mark 16:15)*

This incarnational ministry is the complete opposite of doing things *"in the flesh" (Romans 8:8-9)* (in our own human strength). Incarnational ministry means emulating the ministry of Jesus through complete reliance upon the power of the Holy Spirit.

Unfortunately, in our day, many times incarnational ministry is traded for "tried and true" methods and programs.

No longer do we have to rely on the power of God to do something in us and through us. We can just order a program pack from a Christian book publisher that promises success, or bring in a preacher that can draw a crowd with gimmicks and showmanship. Here's the deal. If we can explain how we did it, then it was not God that accomplished the work but our own ingenuity; that is, the flesh.

The difficulty of this day is that many times we don't even have the opportunity to live incarnationally – to represent Jesus within culture – because we have isolated ourselves from those people that we are supposed to reach by our near-complete immersion in a Christian sub-culture. Additionally, with the modern church's emphasis on activity, people are so programmed to death doing stuff at the church building (and good stuff) that they don't have time to walk in an incarnational ministry outside the walls of their church or home.

Missional – To be missional means that we have been called by God and sent by Him to take His gospel to others. A missional church is different than an attractional church. An attractional church puts on many programs and activities to try to entice those outside of Christ to come in so the "professional" (the preacher or teacher) can tell them about Jesus. The attractional church tries to convince the world that the church is cool, awsome, and totally rad, dude! (Can you tell I grew up in the 80's?)

Is that really our job? To convince others that the church is the "hip" thing to do? I thought that our job was to tell people that Jesus saves…

Church is for believers. Nowhere in the Bible do we find God commanding the unbeliever to go to church to hear the gospel. Instead He commands us to go to them with the gospel. If outsiders come, we will trip over ourselves to make them feel loved and wanted -- and rightly so, but Jesus didn't tell the lost to come to church. He told the individuals that make up the church to go to the lost.

This simple truth takes the pressure off the church that thinks that it has to have all the "latest" in order to look and sound good to the lost. The truth is that the lost man has no desire for church no matter how "current and entertaining" the music, media, and preaching is. When it comes to putting on a show, the church is outmatched by Hollywood. If the lost man wants to see "current and entertaining", he won't go to the church to find it.

So once we discover that it is not our job to "entertain" the lost to Jesus, then we realize that the church is for believers to gather then to go on mission. The mission? Reaching out to unbelievers with the helpful hands and gospel of Jesus. Once the unbeliever becomes a convert, he then will have an appetite for the worship, praise, fellowship, preaching, and teaching that takes place within the walls of the church building.

The missional church minimizes the "required" time of the missionary (read this: church member) at the church building so they can be out among the lost intentionally making contacts and building relationships as platforms to introduce Jesus to others. Each aspect of a truly missional church is designed to equip, and encourage the church member to spend as much time engaging the lost with the gospel and the helping hands of Jesus as possible. This doesn't mean that churches shouldn't have programs or processes within the walls of the building. However, a missional mindset within a church says, "Let's equip and encourage our folks to live each moment on the mission of Jesus. We will treat the church like the connecting hub of the airport instead of the church member's final destination."

This is missional. The church cannot be the end of missions. It must be the means. The mission is always about Jesus and his message to the lost, not about the church.

Organic – An organic church is a church whose schedule, traditions, and practices have been birthed in the culture native to that congregation and "work" for those involved. Unfortunately, most churches today have rigid schedules that reflect an agrarian society that history marched on by a long time ago.

Often congregations (in order to feel good about themselves) stock up on activity at the church building simply for the sake of activity. Each program and church service must be evaluated for value and results. We can't keep doing the same thing over and over and expect different results. In addition to this, the amounts of energy and money expended in ineffective efforts could be refocused to better use in the mission.

The other aspect of an organic church is the concept that it will grow naturally and have some of the character of the people and culture that surround it as did the first-century Jewish and Gentile churches. For example, none of us expect the New York City church to look and feel exactly like the church of Memphis, Tennessee. Why? -- different cultures. The church of the mining town will necessarily look and feel differently than will the church of the farming community. They will have a different schedule, traditions, practices, and in secondary things, they will have different priorities.

It is my belief that each church will function best and accomplish the most for Jesus when they are allowed to experiment and find what works for them, in their situation within the bounds of the Word of God. In truth, the Bible does leave a lot of room for the local church's individual personality and innovation.

Nimble – A church that is bound up by religious red tape is ineffective at best. Each church needs to have simple procedures that can be activated quickly when a situation (read this: opportunity to do something good for Jesus) comes along. So often, good ideas and real needs are tied up in committees and procedures. Because of this, churches never see the good idea implemented or the dire and immediate need met. This means that we are missing hundreds of opportunities to impact our areas and our world for Jesus because of the lack of simplicity in our system.

Let us be clear, a church is not an organization. It is an organism. It has systems not the organizational structures of an institution. Paul calls it **"the body"**. **(First Corinthians 12:12)** Differing from organizational structures, the systems of an organism are efficient. To give an example, my arm and mouth and legs don't have a long conversation about whether they should cooperate to get up and get me a glass of water. It happens pretty quickly.

What is true for the human body remains true for the body of Christ, the church. Simple, organic processes produce a church body that is nimble and responsive to the needs of the community and opportunities that come up to present Jesus. Many times with needs and opportunities you only get one, time-sensitive shot at it. If you miss your window, it won't come around again when the committee finally gets around to making its decision.

If you take time to think about it, these four words describe the first-century church, the church before the box.

- Incarnational – They, by the indwelling of the Spirit of God, displayed the image of Jesus to those around them.
- Missional – They understood that Jesus' last command

was to be their first priority; that they were a sent people who were to live intentionally on mission

- Organic – They had practices, schedules, and traditions that came naturally to them because of the culture in which they lived.
- Nimble - They were free from the organizational chaos, roadblocks, and headaches that slow the modern church to the point of unproductivity.

14. CHURCH MUSIC BEFORE THE BOX

It seems that there is almost nothing more polarizing in the North American church than music. Good men are willing to walk away from each other, not based upon doctrines affecting the gospel, but rather in relation to church music. I use the term "church music" to denote the music that is utilized in the church service. Generally speaking, today's church music falls either into the box of the traditionalist or into the box of commercial Christianity. Both of these boxes are prone to imbalance and intolerance.

The traditionalist church is the one that shuns music simply because it is "new". (If they do use a new song, it has been carefully screened from a narrow list of pre-approved independent publishers.) For the most part, the traditionalist church sticks to the styles of classical, "high church", hymns, and gospel songs. The music is generally (and almost exclusively) played on a piano and organ.

Every now and then when the traditional church really wants to "let its hair down" they will sing a chorus of a gospel song without the verses. They may even go entirely crazy and sing the chorus twice in a row.

On the opposite end of the spectrum, we find another box. This is the box of commercial Christianity. This is the church that is forever singing new music (usually it is just the worship team singing, because no one knows the tune). Generally, the music at a commercial Christian church is chosen because someone bought a CD or downloaded a song played by their favourite Christian band and liked that specific song. Often, not much thought is given to the doctrine of the song or whether the song will fit well with the message from the Bible that week. It is all about the "sound". If a song has the right sound (that being the sound you would hear on the worship leader's favourite radio station), and if the song is popular and is climbing the Christian song charts, you can bet that it will be in the lineup next Sunday.

These two churches are very comfortable in their boxes, and they utterly despise the other box. The traditionalist complains of the "worldly sound" and "lack of doctrine" in the music of the commercialist. The commercialist mocks the traditionalist for being "old fashioned, out of touch, and irrelevant to today." Both camps are entrenched in their box, and it is indicative of how they see their world in other areas as well.

In truth, each extreme of the spectrum has a nugget of truth in its criticism of the other. The traditionalist can be stubborn and slow to make even positive changes. The commercialist can be recklessly permissive in what musical styles and associations he allows in his church. Neither trait is good for a Christian.

But, we have to ask ourselves, "What was it like before the box?" If I may, please let me make some observations.

Instruments: As we look into the Word of God we find dozens of different instruments used to worship God in the temple, to praise God in public victory ceremonies, and unfortunately, used to worship false gods. Nowhere in the Bible, to my knowledge, do we find a specific instrument condemned, and its use prohibited.

As we move into the New Testament, we discover that instruments almost disappear from view. The few times that we observe New Testament saints singing, instruments are nowhere to be found. We do rediscover instruments of string when we get to **Revelation 15:2**. So we do know that there will be, at the very least, "harps" in Heaven.

So does the relative silence concerning instruments in the New Testament mean, as some have surmised, that the church should only sing "a cappella" (without instrumental music)? No, I don't believe so. It is my contention that the writers of Scripture were so busy with evangelism, discipleship, and teaching the great doctrines of the faith that they had little time to devote to squabbling over (or writing about) the instruments which God either approves or disapproves.

Song Writers: In the Bible we find songs written and sung by King David, Moses, Mary and others. While Mary, because little is written of her life, escapes scrutiny we do know that both Moses and David were flawed men. God, however, used flawed men (with, at times, very flawed theology – read some of David's emotional outbursts in the Psalms) to give a nation its music of worship, work, and warfare.

Note: to point out David's flawed theology here is not to indicate that these Psalms (or that any part of Scripture for that matter) is flawed or uninspired. God inspired the inclusion of David's (and others) faulty thinking and reasoning in the Bible in order to show us the weakness of man and the folly of man's best wisdom. (see also some of the statements of Job, Job's friends, and Solomon in the Song of Solomon)

We make this opening statement not to excuse the sins of

these Biblical characters or their modern musical counterparts. We do however, notice that God by His great grace uses flawed and sinful people to accomplish His purposes. In addition , we give credence to the old phrase, "What's good for the goose is good for the gander." Whether they are current writers or those long dead we must use the same criteria by which to determine who we endorse as our song writers. To do anything else opens us up to accusations of hypocrisy.

At each end of the spectrum of Christian music in the modern age, there is faulty thinking in this realm.

The traditionalist would say that he will not use current Christian music because most of it has been written by someone outside of his own theological camp. The inconsistency here lies in the fact that the traditionalist heartily approves of the classical musicians (some, if not many, of whom were totally reprobate) and the writers of hymns and gospel songs which had greatly varying theological views. These views do show up in their music. Especially, if read in the light of the writer's theological perspective. The hymnbook of the traditionalist church is, in truth, very near (if not entirely) ecumenical in its compilation. This produces huge inconsistency in this position.

The commercialist, on the other hand, in his search for the right "sound," very often dismisses the theology (or lack thereof) in a song because it has the "feel" that the worship team is looking for in their "set". This means that, for the commercialist, the message doesn't matter. As long as the writer or performer of the song is popular or is part of a popular band, his music is very desirable to the die-hard commercialist. The problem is this.

When message (theology) is wholly traded for "feel" the purpose of church music is obliterated. That is not to say that church music should not have feeling and emotion. We will tackle this later.

One thing to consider is that the hymnbook, generally speaking, is made up of songs that have become accepted as they have stood the test of popularity over a period of time. So we can't beat up on popularity too much. But current popularity does not necessarily mean longevity, doctrinal correctness, or the approval of God.

The other side of the coin that the commercialist must face is that the music of commercial Christianity has really only been around since the 1960's. This is when record labels began to see the money making opportunity lying dormant in the thousands of North American Christians. It wasn't long before every major secular musician was putting out their own "sacred" album. After artists like Elvis Presley and Johnny Cash that had made their reputation in secular music crossed the line into sacred music with the publication of spiritual albums, church musicians realized that there was money to be made in secular music and began to produce crossover albums that would appeal to both audiences.

(It is important to note here for those within the traditionalist box that "crossover" artists are not new. Even the beloved hymn writer Fanny Crosby[17] wrote both sacred and secular material.)

Since that time, there has been a war over who the church accepts as its song writers. In the end, regardless of whatever side you happen to embrace, a consistent stand is necessary. If the traditionalist will be consistent, he will hold the writers of classical music and hymns to the same standard to which he holds contemporary writers. If the commercialist will be consistent, he will match the theology of the music that he uses to that which is preached from the pulpit of his church and have a well- rounded approach to teaching doctrine with music. Music teaches. The commercialist must grapple with this truth. Check out these verses:

Ephesians 5:19 Speaking to yourselves in psalms and hymns and spiritual songs, singing and making melody in your heart to the Lord;

First Corinthians 14:26 How is it then, brethren? when ye come together, every one of you hath a psalm (<u>a song</u>), hath a doctrine, hath a tongue, hath a revelation, hath an interpretation. <u>Let all things be done unto edifying.</u>

Because music teaches, and because the early believers expected church music to teach and edify (build up), then it has to be about balancing doctrinal correctness with the "feel" or the "sound."

The Sound: To say that there is a particular "sound" of music that God approves of would be disingenuous, intellectually dishonest, and nearly impossible to prove from the Bible. However, we must admit that music is a language of emotion. As such, it is not amoral. By this we mean that the elements of music, notes, rests, rhythm, melody, etc… can be put together like the letters of the alphabet to either spell words of love or curse words. Music then is a moral medium. Music has a moral quality to it, because it is the language of emotion.

The reason we are not just talking about the words of the music is this, God not only cares about what you say, but He also cares how you say it. In speech, our inflection, tone, volume, body language, and facial expression convey as much or more meaning than the words we choose. How then do we give musicians a pass and flippantly say, "Well the words are okay." The words are only a fraction of the total message conveyed. The music itself matters as well.

Here is the tie-in to our Biblical discussion. There are some emotions which the Bible makes clear that Christians are not to indulge themselves. Emotions like greed, unbridled lust, envy, and hate are clearly out of bounds for the Christian. So then, if music is the language of emotion, and there are some emotions that are out of bounds for a Christian to harbor in their lives, then it makes sense that there is music that, simply based upon the emotion that it evokes, is not pleasing to God. When we say "music" here, we are not even talking about the lyrics. Lyrics are easy to approve of or dismiss based on the Bible, the "sound" or "feel" of the music takes more discernment.

The "sound" or "feel" produced when the "letters" of music come together is important because of its powerful impact on the heart. You see, for the most part, music bypasses the intellect and goes straight to the core (heart) of the audience. That makes it an incomparably effective tool for good or evil.

So, what "sound" or "feel" should we allow in the church? Honestly, I don't think there is a good answer for that question. Most of the time, the church "sound" has more to do with the background of the audience and the culture in which they live than any real search as to what God wants. Church music has evolved from plainsong, to Gregorian chant, to the hymns of the Puritans, to the gospel songs of the evangelists, and now to the contemporary Christian music scene (which is not really a genre but a broad term to describe anything that is current and commercially available).

The churches that promote "traditional" music have varying "feels" or "sounds". This variation goes from the puritanical hymn, to bluegrass, country, and folk. The reason that the traditionalist will accept these "sounds" is that he has grown up with them as much of conservative Christianity came out of the culture of the American South. When the southerners (especially the Southern Baptists and the Methodists) began to plant churches elsewhere, their preference and practice was to bring the songs and the "sounds" of the music that they had used in worship for generations and try to graft it onto the indigenous core of the new church, regardless of the cultural differences.

In the end, the "feel" or "sound" of the music itself should be considered as a major factor in its use or abandonment. Not only should one consider whether the song has a current or relevant "vibe," but more importantly, what "feelings" does the music itself evoke? Are those feelings right for a Christian to indulge?

The other part of this picture is the question of association. The sound and feel of a song takes you back to when you first heard that song. Even a similar sounding song can have that effect because it is the sound (not the words) that triggers memory. While unfortunate associations cannot be entirely avoided, (Example: The hymn "Amazing Grace" has been recorded by saint and reprobate alike and performed in places ranging from the church and concert hall to the dive bar on the wrong side of the tracks.) there are certainly some sounds that, while not necessarily ungodly, are unwise for use within the church because of their overwhelmingly strong association with those people, situations, actions, or attitudes that are unhealthy and unbiblical for the Christian.

The last thing to consider concerning the "sound" of the music is who are we trying to glorify? Too often a pianist, organist, guitarist, or drummer will get carried away with showing off what they can do rather than playing for the glory of God and the edification of the congregation. This results in a "sound" that is certainly performance based and performer centered instead of ministry based and Christ centered.

The Audience: Much is made today of "worship", and that is a good thing. We were created to bring glory to the God of Creation. In this section it is important for us to ask, "Who is my audience?" There are those who will say that they have an audience of One – God. That is true, to the extent that we have only One Person we have to <u>please</u> with our music, our Heavenly Father. Another person would point out to the crowd and say, "There's my audience." This also is partially true. A large percentage of the time, the message of the song performed is aimed at the people in the crowd. This is designed to get them to embrace some aspect of the truth of God's Word. The question really comes down to motivation. Is the worship team, instrumentalists, band, choir, or song leader motivated by the crowd or by their King? There is a sincerity that is born out of being motivated by love for Jesus instead of love for attention and applause. Here is a question to ask, "Have I picked out this song because I know the audience likes it, or because it is a part of a message that God wants to be conveyed today?" or "Does the song and the way I sing it give others the idea that I am interested in the praise of me or the praise of God?"

Who we sing for is vitally more important that what or how we sing, because it is the WHO that determines the what or how.

The debate will continue to rage among those that are determined to stay within their box and drag others into the confines of their cardboard cell as well. However, for those that wish to be free of the box on either end of the spectrum my suggestion is the following: Each individual church has the God given right, responsibility, and authority to search the Scriptures and apply them to the area of music while prayerfully seeking what God wants for the music that is utilized within their congregation.

While embracing that right and responsibility for our own

local church, we must avoid pressuring others to walk in lockstep with us in their musical choices. The deep thought here is this; if I am using the threat (either spoken or implied) of "unfriending" a church to get them to walk the way I do in regard to music, are they then following the leading of Jesus, or are they following me?

Yes, you can line up fifty different pastors and church musicians, and you will get fifty different ideas about what good church music is. The problem between churches in regard to music comes in to play in cooperative efforts. It is this moment that calls pastors and musicians to give up the prideful posturing of their position on the matter and be statesmen. Compromise of conviction is not necessary, but humble communication and discussion as to what can be done to mitigate offense and maximize potential good is necessary.

Music in the church is a difficult ministry. Like the church nursery or the kitchen, there are a multitude of opportunities for conflict. Don't go near it unless you have thick skin and the padding of an NHL goalie. Everyone thinks that they are an expert, and everyone (even the tone deaf grandpa) has an opinion.

Because the Bible only sets out general guidelines and principles that we can apply to music and does not nail down the "Thou Shalt / Thou Shalt Not" in specific musical terms this will be an ongoing conversation. To further complicate the issue, each believer tends to read into and take from the Bible ideas about music that are more based upon their own preference or culture rather than conclusions based upon what the actual words of the Bible say. Well, this will be debated until Jesus comes back. But until then, let's make sure that it is a humble, civil conversation, not a shouting match between factions entrenched in their boxes.

15. CHURCH LEADERSHIP EXPECTATIONS BEFORE THE BOX

What was ministry like before the box? As we look at the early church up to the modern era, we find that expectations of the players within the church ministry were wholly different than the expectations of today. It is this expectations game that has plunged so many in the ministry into confusion, disappointment, and despair. This expectations game is a killer of many good men and women.

The Pastor/Elder– In the beginning, the role of the pastor was pretty straightforward. His job was to teach/preach Scripture, oversee the function of the congregation, and live a life that was representative of Jesus so others could follow. The thing is, he wasn't doing this alone. As a matter of fact, most times in the early church we find multiple people working harmoniously to lead a church.

In chapter six, we talked about the team approach to missions work. The ministry at home is no different. No man has all of the skills necessary to do all that needs to be done in leading the local church. Whether you call them pastors and assistant/associate pastors or you call them lead elders, teaching elders and administrative elders, it all boils down to the word "TEAM".

Of course, there is always the team leader. This is the guy that everyone naturally looks to when there is a problem to solve or a project to tackle. We find in the Bible that God placed men into particular situations because of their qualification and their giftings. These men were looked to and relied upon by others for leadership. God works in and through people. Unfortunately, in many ways the term "leader" has been misdefined as "sole authority" within the church as if the pastor/elder was president instead of a servant. This has led to power struggles within the church and to egos the size of Texas. When one sees himself as a leader among a team of leaders he sees himself in the light of the New Testament.

Now, it is clear that there are small churches that only have one individual that is qualified and gifted to be a pastor/elder. This is not a break from Scriptural norm, but instead should be seen as a precursor to it. The congregation should be looking toward and preparing for the day when they can add to the leadership team. This addition of qualified individuals will dramatically expand the impact of that congregation for Christ in their community.

The other box that the modern pastor/elder faces is the expectations box. The expectation in our modern day is that the pastor must be all things to all men, and that is just not possible. One man cannot (and is not called to) be the executive, the cool guy, the orator, the fun guy, the visitation guy, the church custodian, and handyman. In *Acts 6:4*, the apostles told the church to choose men to take care of some physical needs of the congregation so that they (the apostles) could devote their time to prayer and ministry of the Word of God. The Biblical church has Biblical expectations for those on their leadership team.

The Pastor's Wife – It is strange in the light of history that we should even have to have this section in the book. Before the box, the pastor's wife was just that; the pastor's wife.

Unfortunately, with the increasingly authoritative model of the pastorate and the desire of the church to meet the expectations of the feminist movement, a new (although unofficial) position was christened within the church, that of THE PASTOR'S WIFE. I've watched churches lift up this newly formed "position" in the church to the point that decisions were routinely run through the pastor's wife rather than the duly elected and God-called leadership team of the church.

With the initiation of this exalted position within the church (some churches even call their pastor's wife "The First Lady of the Church") came a whole slew of unBiblical expectations that churches dumped upon unsuspecting ladies that were just trying to love and support their preacher husbands. Biblically, the responsibility of the pastor's wife is to be a good and loving wife and mother and to serve Jesus in whatever aspects of ministry in which the Holy Spirit leads her to be involved. When people ask me, "What does your wife do in the church?" I answer, "Her job is to take care of me and do whatever else Jesus asks her to do."

You see, what many churches are looking for is not a pastor/elder, but what they call a "ministry couple". This (with the possible exception of Priscilla and Aquilla in *Acts 18*) is wholly out of the norm of Biblical church leadership. For the vast majority of churches in New Testament times, we hear next to nothing about the spouse of the pastor/elder.

We do not say this to indicate that the wife of the pastor/elder is incapable of being a strong partner in ministry or is undesirable for service within ministry in some way. (We all are to find places of service within the church.) In fact, most of the wives of pastors and elders are beautiful, talented, educated women who serve Christ in any number of ways in and through their local church. Our contention is that the church should not expect that the wife of the pastor/elder be the one who plays the instruments for worship, plans the potlucks, teaches the women's classes, goes to visit the sick, dresses like she stepped out of a magazine, and sings like an angel.

Now, bless God for those women who have those abilities and those callings, but let's not dump those unbiblical expectations upon the wife of God's servant. She will have enough on her plate, because God will use her to help keep your pastor/elder's head screwed on straight and his priorities in check. She will encourage him when he is down, and at times she may be the only person willing to speak truth to him. You desperately need her to be the wife of the pastor, but there is no need in the church for the office of the Pastor's Wife. Simply put, she is the wife of the pastor, not the wife of the congregation.

The Deacon and the Wife of the Deacon - Much of what we have already addressed concerning the pastor/elder and his wife can be said about the deacon and the lady he married. God has placed the deacon in the church to be a servant and to help the congregation pursue the vision and mission entrusted to them by God. I am thankful for the great deacons and their lovely wives that I have had the privilege of knowing and working alongside these many years.

The truth is that the expectations game is one that will never entirely leave the church. However, it is incumbent upon us as leaders to have Biblical expectations for ourselves, our spouses, our children and the leaders around us. Far too often the congregation has unrealistic and harmful expectations because a pastor/elder has communicated those same expectations to them. Too many good leaders have found themselves trapped in a box of their own making when it comes to expectations.

If you find that you are currently in a situation where the expectations are onerous and above the call of Scripture there are some things you can do.

First, realize that just because it has been done and has been expected in the past doesn't make it right.

Second, get before the God of all comfort and ask what He expects.

Third, begin slowly and methodically bringing some of the Scriptural principles regarding this topic into your teaching and private conversation. Don't drop a bomb, but rather dispense a little crumb here and there. People most often change their minds about things when they think it is their idea.

Fourth, call in some outside help. Find another brother that has a balanced view on this topic (and a track record to back it up) and ask him to come in and share his experiences with your leadership team and congregation. Many times hearing the same thing from another source will get people to think.

If we are not careful, the box of expectations can quickly become a prison. But the best way to be free is not to get into jail in the first place. When you are looking into a new ministry, be sure that their expectations do not overreach either Scripture or your abilities. Allow honesty and good, common sense to prevail and God will lead you to the place where you best fit.

16. INNOVATION BEFORE THE BOX

We are a culture that is absolutely in love with what is "new," "hip," and "happening." Whether it is the latest gadget, song, or bit of gossip from some celeb's life, we eat it up.

As for me, I like useful innovation. I like fire. I like the wheel. I like fried chicken and the horseless carriage (an early name for the automobile). However, innovation for innovation's sake alone is a problem.

Here it is. There are, (as we have previously discussed) in most instances, two very imbalanced positions or "boxes" when it comes to spiritual matters. When it comes to the topic of innovation, we find no exception.

The first box we will tackle is the box that despises innovation or change simply upon the basis that it is "new." For those that occupy this box, the traditions and methods that surround their faith have become so interwoven with it that to change is (to them) heretical. For this group the mere concept of innovation tears at the fabric of what they believe about themselves and their faith.

We find pockets of this thinking (to varying degrees) in each of the tribes and denominations. From the Amish in their buggies, to the Baptist church organ that, "We have to use because Aunt Gertrude donated it forty years ago," every group has its dyed in the wool traditionalists for whom change is anathema.

To get this group to begin to peek out of their box, let's look "before the box" to Jesus. Jesus was a game changer. The religious establishment had their ideas and traditions, and some of them were pretty good! As a matter of fact, Jesus Himself followed all of the Jewish laws perfectly until His own death. Jesus, by means of His death and resurrection, fulfilled the law and completely did away with the need for the traditions to which they had clung. That doesn't mean that laws and traditions were wrong, but it does mean that God was doing something new. Later, it was Peter and Paul that God shook loose of the traditions of their upbringing to lead in the acceptance of the Gentiles into the church.

The truth is that the churches of North America have been on a journey of change from the moment that the Pilgrims landed. They, who were looking for religious freedom themselves, set the tone for the Anabaptist and Non-Conformist / Protestant churches of the New World. In framing the government of this new land, the founders said that religion was the right of the individual not the right of the state.

As a result, the United States differed from Europe in that it specifically avoided having a specific state sponsored religion with codified traditions and methods. From that point on, the idea of the individual's right to worship God as his conscience dictated became imbedded in the psyche of North American Christianity. Because of this new concept in civil governance, North American churches became, over the years, a hotbed of innovation.

But not all Christian groups welcome innovation. Many find great comfort, protection, and identity in their traditions. (I do have to pause here and ask whether it is a good thing to find identity in our traditions rather than in Jesus. I think we know the answer, right?)

There are dozens of methods and traditions that have become deeply entwined with the identity of those within the "anti-change" (I use this term lovingly) box. This is the very reason that the phrase "sacred cow" began to be applied to those non-essential things that churches refuse to change. For those good folks, to change would be to deny who they are as believers.

May I gently say this? If God wants us to stay the same, why does he command us to grow? *(Second Peter 3:18)* Is it possible for us to grow to any real extent without our methods, traditions, and understanding being challenged? Does spiritual growth somehow happen without eventually affecting our methods and traditions? Can we honestly follow Jesus in a transformative way without being transformed *(Romans 12:2)* in every area? In the end, every part of our worship, work, and warfare for Christ has to be considered in light of the character of Christ, the mission of God, and the people to whom we minister. This evaluation, at times, will recognize deficiencies in ourselves and changes in those around us that necessitate innovation.

Now, whatever your feelings are about the changing face of the church, we have to agree that the freedom to innovate and change is something that we all would defend. Whether or not you want to change is not the point. The point is we all want (and we have) the freedom to change if God points us in that direction.

Moving right along, we look at the box on the other end of

the pendulum swing. For those that make this box their home, change comes as easy as changing their socks, and it is sought after and anticipated like a child waits impatiently for ice cream to be scooped out of the bucket. Each new book, new course, new song, new band, new teacher, new church, new church model, or new ministry is latched onto like some kind of adolescent fiend on a candy high.

For these well-meaning but inwardly turbulent Christians, change itself and the means of change (the new book, preacher, course, etc...) becomes an idol. With the rabid adoption of each new innovation comes the belief that it will "fix" things. This was a trap that I fell into in my early ministry. For some reason, I was just convinced that if I could just get this new hymnbook, that new Sunday school material, or the newest church promotional package that it would create the breakthrough in ministry that I desired for the church. Yeah, that didn't work. Why? God didn't want a new hymnbook, Sunday school material, or promotional idea to get the credit for building His church! That is His job, and He is very jealous of it. He wants us totally dependent upon Himself for everything...because we are.

To rely on innovation to "fix" the individual or the church puts the change and the means of change in the place of a saviour in our lives.

So, in truth, that new ministry model, method, or idea is what this group looks to repair or rejuvenate what they see as wrong in themselves or their church. This leaves Jesus in some kind of secondary role. The scary thing is that much of consumer Christianity is unconsciously built upon the creation of these functional saviours (idols) taking the place of Jesus. After all, it is so much easier to buy a new product or hire a new speaker than it is to consistently build a relationship with God and wait on Him for the "fix" that we need. We don't need the newest thing, we need Jesus. He and He alone must be the One we look to for repair and rejuvenation.

The Bible speaks of those that have this "if it is new, it must be good" attitude. *(Second Timothy 4:3 and Ephesians 4:14)* It talks of a group of people who are "tossed" to every new idea and are piling up teachers because their ears "itch" for new ideas.

For those in this box, the word "old" has become a pejorative (derogatory) term that they use to put down anything that smacks of tradition. If they desire to cast derision on an idea, they frame it as coming from an "old white man". Apparently, Caucasian men lose their ability to have good ideas somewhere around forty years of age. I wasn't aware that this was the case (and it is not), but as I watch and listen to the media that is the idea that is conveyed. Aged white men just aren't cool, so any ideas they may have – in church or in culture at large – are, by and large, ignored.

Along with the idol of "new" most often comes the idolatry of youth. In the 1960's, the saying was, "Don't trust anyone over thirty." The baby boom generation now are grandparents and they missed some very important lessons that their "old" mentors were trying to impart in the 1960's. Even more frightening is the fact that these baby boomers have for years been the heads of almost every major corporation and educational institution in the country. Is it any wonder (given their adoration of their own youthful ideas and radical ideology in the 1960's) that the baby boomers have moved from making executive decisions to asking the younger generation, "What do you think?" "What do you want?" So you see how the baby boom generation has moved from an idolization of their own youth and youthful ideas to idolizing the youth of today.

There is no place in society that this is more blatant than in the church. In many cases, the older generation of those that are living in the "must have innovation" box are willing to throw away nearly everything within the church to satisfy yet another generation's fascination with change and innovation.

To bring this topic of innovation to a conclusion, let's look at a balanced approach to change.

Change is part of life. If you stop changing, you stop living. It is the same in the church. When I go back to the church I grew up in, I find dozens of changes of varying in size and importance. It is the same church, but it has made allowances to minister to a different ethnic population and a new economic demographic that has moved into the area, has a new pastor, has new décor, etc… For every church, the old saying "adapt or die" is a truism. We must, however, make sure that we are not looking to some innovation as our savior from church decay or decline.

Balanced with that, we must not become change addicts that begin to look at all of tradition as something that must be done away with. Tradition is good. It brings people together and is part of the social glue that holds groups together. The church's annual Christmas dinner, the men's fishing trip, the Mother's Day tea are those shared events that, like Christmas, cement shared memories, and that is good and necessary.

Change can't just be about the change itself. Change has to be about God. We have to be able to say, "God wants this." That means that change has to be entered upon with great prayer and serious study.

Because of this, the implementation of change is not for the young or for those young in the faith. Although these two groups have, many times, the drive and enthusiasm to carry out change, they generally lack several essential ingredients to make change successful. Those ingredients are:

- ***Context*** – seeing the big picture is part of the job of the elder statesmen of the church. Wise leaders will see the interconnections within the congregation that are affected by change.
- ***Wisdom*** – is the proper application of knowledge. Sometimes it is not the change itself, but its presentation, implementation, and timing that cause trouble.
- ***Commitment*** – the ability to faithfully stick to a plan and see it through to fruition is a quality of the mature person/believer. Youthful enthusiasm may be sufficient to point out a problem, but it is totally inadequate to identify a solution and see its implementation through to a satisfactory conclusion.

Warren Wiersbe[11] in his book "On Being a Servant of God" tells us not to take down a fence until we understand why it was put there in the first place. This is the trouble with youthful enthusiasm for innovation. Most times, the youth that seek change haven't taken the time to understand why things are the way they are in the first place. An understanding of history and rationale is necessary if one wishes to change the present for the better.

Change is inevitable and profitable, but change is never the solution nor the goal. Jesus is.

17. DISCIPLESHIP BEFORE THE BOX

In nearly every church that I have ever visited, read about, or heard about, discipleship goes something like this:

Pastor: "Hey! I'm glad you are here!"

Visitor: "Pastor, I need to talk to you. I have recently come to know Jesus as my Saviour and am looking for a church to call home."

Pastor: "That's fantastic. What about our church?"

Visitor: "Yeah, that's kind of why I'm talking to you."

Pastor: "Oh."

Embarrassment and bewilderment clouds his brain for a second.

"This never happens." He thinks to himself.

Shaken back to reality, he realizes the visitor is still talking to him.

"So, what do I need to do to get baptized and become a member?"

At this point, the pastor's arm involuntarily comes up and slaps his face.

"I have to wake up," he thinks. "This has to be a dream. Did they really say they want to be a part of THIS church?"

Well, the slap to the face was enough to convince him that he is indeed awake, and that there is a real, live person who wants to be a part of THIS church. After his initial shock starts to wear off, he begins to explain the church's membership or discipleship process. In most churches, these two things are seen as one item (not necessarily a good thing) that must be checked off before one can be inducted into membership in the church.

The process varies wildly from church to church and between tribes and denominations, but generally what is called "discipleship" today is little more than some lessons on Bible doctrine and church practice. Once the new convert (or membership candidate) has completed these lessons, he or she is deemed to have been "discipled", and that's the extent of it.

The goal of the specific church, of course, is to make sure that the person who desires to be baptized or become a member is "indoctrinated" (nobody uses or likes that word but it's the right one) with the Biblical teachings and practices of that specific church. This may be indoctrination; it may be teaching. It is a part of discipleship, but it is not the whole of Biblical discipleship.

In this short chapter, we really are going to do nothing more than scratch the surface of discipleship and start a conversation. That conversation has already been played out in dozens of books dedicated to the topic. For now, however, let's pretend that those other books don't exist and ask ourselves. What was discipleship like before the box?

In the Bible, the word "disciple" conveys the idea of a learner, a pupil, or one who is taught. Having established this, let's try to understand how this teaching and learning played out in the first-century church.

Jesus, our ultimate example, had some disciples who eventually became apostles and, after His death and resurrection, the leaders of the movement. He called them from their various trades. Then He spent between two and three years with them, walking, talking, eating, playing, and yes, instructing. In Jesus we see that the discipleship process looks more like mentorship and less like a classroom or lessons from a book. Because Christianity is about a Person, Jesus wanted those men with Him to watch the way He handled Himself, to hear his speech, and by this, to understand His heart. Yes, along the way they learned deep and heavy doctrinal truth, but it was in the context of relationship and mentoring in real life environment.

North America has only half- heartedly accepted the notion of mentoring. We like to do our mentoring like speed dating. We quit what we are doing in our "real lives" and go somewhere to meet the person we are supposed to be mentoring. Then we sit down with a coffee and say, "Ok, I have an hour. Sit down with me and I will mentor you." This isn't the example that Jesus portrayed. He invited others into His life, and they learned as they walked, worked, played, and prayed together.

The problem is that our society is becoming more and more insular and individualistic. Our homes, and by extension our lives, are not welcoming. Instead, our homes have become our brick fortresses that protect us from others while we watch the lives of others on television and follow them on the internet. As warped as it sounds, our society would rather develop emotional attachments to fictional characters on television and reality TV stars than build lasting genuine relationships with real people.

Here's the core of the issue; don't miss it. Simply put, you cannot mentor (read this: disciple) anyone if you can't let them into your life at least a little bit. Jesus, our example, had a no-holds-barred approach to accessibility except when He went into the mountaintop to spend time with His Father.

Before the box of North American "efficiency", things happened at a much slower pace. True discipleship and mentoring came naturally to the believers because they did not simply attend the same church. They, as the church, lived life together. They shared the ups, the downs, the joys, and the sorrows of life together. This does not mean that they lived in a compound community up in the hills away from everyone else, nor does it mean that they lived with their noses in everyone else's business. It does mean, however, that they were deeply invested in each other's lives, and deeply concerned with the success of their brother or sister in Christ. This is the kind of practical love that Jesus expected others to see in the community of Christians that we call the church. *(John 13:35)*

We often bemoan the fact that there are so many spectators in the church pews and not enough believers actually pulling their weight in ministry. Much of this can be traced back to the DNA that was embedded into them during their own discipleship. If the congregation that discipled them gave them a book on doctrine, a copy of the Daily Bread devotional, and ten weeks of class time with the pastor in a membership candidates class, then you get a disciple who thinks that the Christian life is about learning the right answers and showing up. If someone from that same congregation opens up their life and shows that convert by their words, actions, and attitude how to walk like Jesus in real life, the result is a disciple that realizes that the Christian life is not about the answers, but about walking with a Person and serving Him each day. This is how we move people off of the benches onto the playing field that is the Christian life. This is the core of discipleship "before the box."

CONCLUSION

Between North and South Korea is a strip of land called the "Demilitarized Zone" or DMZ. On each side of this section of land is an army with its guns sighted in on those who are on the other side of the DMZ. It is tragically unfortunate, but there are deep emotional, political, and historical reasons that this is the case.

Unfortunately, in many cases, good Christian churches have done the same thing in retreating to a box on one or the other end of the field where a battle once took place. There they have declared that their position in the field, their box, is the right box. So each side has, like the troops of World War One, dug down and become entrenched in their thinking, methods, practices, and traditions. Very little thought is given to what God wants, but much effort is expended in keeping the status-quo and maintaining a certain image and position for the others within their denomination or tribe.

With armies amassed in their boxes on each end of the field, there are a few brave souls that understand that there is inconsistency within each box that is entirely unbiblical and completely avoidable while staying within the box. The perplexing truth, however, is that those who do not choose a box have to live in the DMZ. There, they run the hazard of being shot by those on either side of any issue.

In this fractious age within Christianity, it is easy to follow the call of those within the boxes to "take a stand with us" – even if that stand is not logical, consistent, or Biblical. It is much more difficult to look at the Word of God and ask ourselves, "I wonder what it was like before the box?"

I wish I could have lived in that first-century church. It was a church that was raw and vibrant, a church without ingrained expectations and boxes. There wasn't time for it. They were running for their lives and spreading the message of Jesus! There was no box to fit into, so they didn't have to pretend that the box actually fit! They didn't have a box; they had a leader: Jesus. They were honest in that they were sincerely trying to "figure it out" as they went. And for them, that was enough. Mistakes would be made, but they would be sincere mistakes as they sought to be transformed into the image of Jesus and to further His cause.

I believe that God is most pleased when we seek His will for our churches and our lives while completely ignoring the boxes that church tradition, church culture, and the expectations of others have imposed upon us. If we sincerely follow Him and honestly seek the truth of Scripture, we may not be understood by others, but we will please Him. And that is more than enough.

SO WHAT DO I DO NOW?

As we said in the introduction, this book is not about a new church model nor is it about finding some "nugget" that will make your current church model purr along like the engine of a Ferrari. Church culture as a whole in North America is not going forward, but sideways. It is the contention of this author that backward is the right direction in which to go. As you consider the best way for you to implement the "Before the Box" approach here are some ideas to consider.

ONE: Do not throw everything out and try to start everything again from scratch. Much of what we do is grounded in Scripture and supported by history. In addition to this essentially Biblical core that has been handed down to us we also have churches and other infrastructure (like educational and missions institutions) that may need to be tweaked – even more than tweaked, but to tear them down to rebuild would be a supreme act of pride and would discount the good work of those who have come before us.

One man said that every step forward begins with one foot firmly planted in the past. This is true. We have to research, understand, and come to grips with history before we can understand ourselves and make the necessary alterations to emulate first-century practice. Too many zealous people grab one idea from a book or seminar and try to use that single thought to completely revamp their church and ministry.

Ministry renewal is not about the one idea that you are excited about. Instead (from a human effort perspective) it is a lot of buttons and knobs and levers that all have to be pushed, turned, and pulled just the right amount, in just the right sequence, at just the right time. It is in this complicated "tuning" that we find the strategy of "Before the Box." This is where we have to rely upon the Holy Spirit to give us the wisdom that was given to Solomon. If, in enthusiasm, we try to ditch all of what we are used to in order to start over, we will find ourselves with some ideas but without the buttons, knobs, and levers that we need. Doctrine, history, tradition, practice, churches, and institutions must not be unilaterally abandoned, but instead must be Biblically examined and radical changes soaked in the marinade of patience, love, and nuance must be implemented.

TWO: There are things you can begin to do without tearing anything down.

There is a part in all real men that loves to watch those shows on television that show demolition crews imploding huge buildings. From setting the charges, to flipping the switch, to that moment the building collapses in a thundering cloud of dust, we can't get enough of it.

Church life is different. If you blow it up, you hurt people. That's not good. So, start with the positive things. Gain your followers' trust in the changes that are of a positive nature first. Here are some ideas to get you started.

- Start "doing good." Look for people that have a need and do what you can to meet that need.
- Invite a new convert into your life to mentor them.
- Get to know your missionaries. You communicate with them. Make them feel important and special...because they are!

THREE: Do not try to tackle it all at once. Most of us are not good at juggling all of the ministry aspects that we do well, much less the ones we struggle with. So, we should not think that we are able to make more than one change at once. If you make one change that becomes a positive experience for you and those around you, you will gain more of your followers' trust. Every leader has a finite measure of "political capital" to spend. If you do one thing well, you will gain more of that capital. However, if you try to do a lot of things at once, chances are that you will become a leader that is bankrupt in that department.

FOUR: Pray consistently about what God would have you change or discard. In this prayer process, take your time. It has taken you years to get where you are, and it is reasonable to take some months or years to turn the ship around. Change is a necessary part of growth, but change without deliberate thought and implementation does damage.

FIVE: When the Lord has impressed on you a change you need to implement, be patient with those who are affected by that change. Meet with them (formally or informally) and explain what you plan to do. Listen to their concerns and ideas. They have value. Pay close attention to those people who are reticent about change. Try to understand where they are coming from. In the end, they may have to be dragged into positive change kicking and screaming. However, usually some quiet conversations, an acknowledgement of history and tradition, time, and a patient spirit will alleviate their concerns.

SIX: Do not become a crusader for your change, strategy, or idea. It has taken you time to come to the conclusions, and opinions you now hold. Give others the time and liberty to make these changes or totally different ones in their own time, as the Lord leads.

SEVEN: Do not expect "instant" results. Quality takes time. In addition, the work of God is just that, a work of God.

He (and His timing) is the determining factor.

As we have noted, this is not a plug and play book. Although we have necessarily made reference to specific ideas in order to establish a frame of reference for a bigger macro discussion, simply putting into place the changes that we have mentioned in examples will not guarantee success…instant or otherwise.

EIGHT: It is your ability to consistently think and act within a Biblical framework that will ultimately bring the renewal you seek. The specific changes that you may implement are the trees, but in this book we have tried to lift our eyes above the trees to see the big picture of the forest. The "forest" truth of "Before the Box" is this: We will never attain the ideal that we seek, but direction and progress is success.

NINE: Become part of the conversation! This book is has not been intended to be a final product, but rather a framework to assist in the ongoing conversation that, God willing, will draw us out of our boxes and closer to the Biblical ideal. Go to www.facebook.com/beforethebox or www.beforethebox.org and become part of the ongoing conversation as we walk together on this journey.

Final Note: *This book has been years in the making and that formation is still taking place. If, after reading this entire book you have constructive criticism or thoughts regarding additions that may make the second edition better I would be glad to have your input. – Jason Homan*

END NOTES

1. Dr. Charles Keen – First Bible International www.firstbible.net/charleskeen.html
2. Encyclopedia of 77,000 Illustrations, Paul Lee Tan, 1984, Pg. 862
3. 1 Thessalonians 2:4; 1 Corinthians 4:51; Samuel 16:7; Hebrews 4:12
4. Henry Martyn (1781-18120 - Anglican minister and missionary to the people of India and Persia
5. John 10:10; Romans 12:2; 2 Corinthians 5:17
6. James Strong (1822 –1894) was a Methodist Biblical scholar and educator
7. Edward McKendree Bounds - (1835 – 1913) author, attorney, clergyman of Methodist Episcopal Church
8. Norman Percy Grubb - (1895 – 15 1993) missionary, writer and Bible teacher
9. Robert Reynolds Jones, Sr. - (1883 – 1968) evangelist, religious broadcaster, founder and first president of Bob Jones University
10. Francis of Assisi (c. 1182 –1226) Italian Catholic leader who founded the Order of Friars Minor, more commonly known as the Franciscans
11. Warren W. Wiersbe is an American pastor, Bible teacher, conference speaker and a prolific writer Born: May 16, 1929, East Chicago, Indiana, United States
12. Bryan Chapell (PhD, Southern Illinois University) is president and professor of practical theology at Covenant Theological Seminary in St. Louis, where he has served in various capacities since 1984.
13. John Richard Rice (December 11, 1895 – December 29, 1980) was a Baptist evangelist and pastor and the founding editor of The Sword of the Lord, an influential fundamentalist newspaper.
14. Charles Andrew "Andy" Stanley (born May 16, 1958) is

the senior pastor of North Point Community Church near Atlanta Georgia

15. Thom S. Rainer (born July 16, 1955) is the president and CEO of LifeWay Christian Resources.
16. Eric Geiger serves as one of the Vice Presidents at LifeWay Christian Resources, leading the Church Resources Division.
17. Frances Jane van Alstyne Crosby (March 24, 1820 – February 12, 1915), more commonly known as Fanny Crosby, was an American mission worker, poet, lyricist, and composer. A lifelong Methodist, she was one of the most prolific hymnists in history.

GLOSSARY

- Application – using the direct commands and principles found in the Bible to impact attitudes, ideas, decisions, and action
- Anathema – accursed, banned
- Balance – a situation in which different elements are equal or in the correct proportions.
- Box – that which confines a church not allowing Biblical latitude, diversity, or consistency
- Christendom – used in a historical sense, the time period from the medieval to the modern period, during which the Christian world represented a cultural, geopolitical power
- Christianity – those who have truly received salvation from Jesus by grace through faith alone
- Christianity (broader) – all those who claim to follow Jesus as Saviour, any church claiming to be "Christian"
- Conservative – those whose beliefs about the faith compel them to very slow, or no progression or change in practice, methodology, and tradition
- Consistency – the ability to approach every situation or problem with the same set of criteria
- Core Doctrines – those doctrines which directly impact the Gospel, and would irrevocably change Christianity if altered or deleted
- Culture – the ideas, customs, arts, and social behavior of a particular people group
- Cultural Christian – an individual that supports the church by means of attendance and finance because that is what is expected of him by society and is advantageous to him
- Denomination - a subgroup within a religion that

operates under a common name, tradition, and identity
- Devotions – a quiet time with God usually comprised of Bible reading, meditation on Scripture, and prayer
- Evangelicalism – those Christian churches, associations, and denominations that are orthodox in their theology and are actively pursuing the conversion of others to Christianity
- Ecclesiastical - relating to the Christian Church or its clergy
- Ecumenical – involving people from different kinds of Christian (in the broadest possible sense) churches with no regard to agreement on orthodox or core doctrine
- Fasting – to refrain from the consumption of food for the purpose of focusing upon that which is spiritual
- Heretical – The Bible's use of the word "heretic" carries the idea of someone that is schismatic, someone who is trying to drive a wedge between and draw people away. The use of the word "heretic" in this book utilizes the more popular definition. That is, one who has denied the core of the Christian faith.
- Hypocrisy - the practice of claiming to have higher standards or more noble beliefs than is the case or condemning in another what is present in one's self
- Inner Spiritual Life – the individual's private walk with God
- Interpretation – the act of explaining the direct, explicit meaning of Scripture as opposed to the application of that Scripture extrapolated from that meaning
- Kingdom of Darkness – that which in the physical and spiritual realm is under the control of satan
- Liberalism – those churches, associations, and denominations that have been willing to alter, ignore, or deny orthodox theology/core doctrine
- Local Church – the individual congregation in a certain

specific geographic location

- Meditate – to think upon or ponder one thing (in this case Scripture)
- Methods – those means which a church employs to accomplish its goals
- Motive – the inner reasons of why an individual engages in a specific action or attitude
- Native – that which naturally grows in a given geographic area or climate
- Orthodox Theology – that core, historically agreed upon, theological position that comprises those teachings which are foundational to the function of the Gospel without which a church is no longer considered to be Biblically sound
- Para-Church Organization – Christian faith-based organization that works outside of and across denominations to engage in social welfare and evangelism, usually independent of local church oversight
- Praise – the joyful expression of the heart toward God in appreciation for who He is and what He does
- Program – a plan enacted on a regular basis that involves effort, money, and personnel which is intended to accomplish a specific goal
- Progressive – those whose concept of the faith's relationship with culture forces them to adapt their church to the trends and thought of society
- Promotion - the publicizing of a product, organization, or venture so as to increase public awareness
- Quiet Time – that time that an individual spends with God alone
- Sanctification – set apart for a higher purpose – in this book, progressive sanctification, each day being set apart a little bit more for and to God impacting thought, attitude, and action

- Secondary Issue – those topics upon which Bible believing individuals disagree; topics that don't impact the definition or operation of the Gospel
- Sub-culture - a cultural group within a larger culture, often having beliefs or interests at variance with those of the larger culture
- Traditions – those practices within the church that are not part of the commands of Scripture
- Tribe – any group of churches that have banded together or are connected by common doctrine, traditions, and practice
- Worship – the complete submission of a life to God and the actions and attitudes that emanate from that submission – worship always involves the sacrifice of something and serving something or some one

ABOUT THE AUTHOR

Jason Homan spent his early years among the corn fields of Michigan, USA and as a teenager enjoyed the bustling suburbs of Toronto, Ontario, Canada. He grew up in the home of a missionary pastor and trusted Jesus Christ as his personal Saviour while still a child. Upon graduation from high school Jason enrolled in FaithWay Baptist College of Canada earning a Bachelor of Theology degree. Shortly after graduation Jason married his college sweetheart, Debbie. Following this, God allowed them to work together in some of the most dynamic ministries in Canada. In the summer of 2000 God led them to Cape Breton Island and Northside Baptist. It has been their privilege to love and be loved by the people of that church since that time.

Presently Jason divides his time between pastoring, writing, and speaking engagements. When not "working" (He doesn't think of ministry as work.) he can be found tinkering with his old truck or plucking away on his guitar.

More about Jason Homan at www.jasonhoman.com

33717546R00088

Made in the USA
Middletown, DE
19 January 2019